MANUSCRIPT WRITING USING ENDNOTE AND WORD

A User's Guide that Makes Your Scientific Writing Easier

By Bengt M. Edhlund

LIMITED LIABILITY

This document describes the functions and features valid for Word 97 in combination with EndNote 7 and Word 2000, 2002 or 2003 in combination with EndNote 7, 8, 9, or X. Form & Kunskap is unable to predict or anticipate changes in service performance or functionality of later versions or changes of respective software that might influence or change the described features.

FORM & KUNSKAP AB • P.O.BOX 4 • SE-640 61 STALLARHOLMEN • SWEDEN • +46 152-201 80
SALES@FORMKUNSKAP.COM • WWW.FORMKUNSKAP.COM

ISBN 978-1-4116-8839-1

MANUSCRIPT WRITING USING ENDNOTE AND WORD

EndNote is a reference handling software that offers benefits to writers in virtually any science or discipline. The main purpose of such software is to transfer literature references from external sources to the user in such a way that he or she may use them instantly in the word processor while writing. However, the existence of external sources or scientific databases that can deliver data to EndNote by means of search and retrieval varies largely between sciences. Each science has its own set of problems, opportunities and limitations.

This book focuses on manuscript handling, which comprises of the common procedures for various disciplines which we define as the combined use of EndNote, Word and the integrated function Cite While You Write or CWYW.

Emphases on main features and functions together with recommendations for practical settings and other guidelines is the landmark for this literature. The author has collected experience from many years training courses and lectures given at numerous universities and within the industry.

While the material is built up as course literature and has a character of an encyclopedia it also serves well as material for self-studies.

TABLE OF CONTENTS

1. INTRODUCTION

This book gives the reader an overview of the main functions and features of EndNote: how to create an EndNote Library with references, and how to handle and organize them. The reader will then come to understand more deeply the combined use of EndNote and Word so that manuscripts including literature references will follow author instructions set up by publishers or others.

Methods for importing data for specific user groups that are dependent on certain access to public or commercial scientific databases are dealt with separately for each science or discipline in other literature also available from Form & Kunskap.

Therefore this book focuses on the function related to manuscript handling and the features that EndNote creates in Word: Cite While You Write or CWYW. Even though EndNote incorporates a large number of Output Styles, which are interpretations of author instructions for citing references usually related to a certain scientific journal or known norms, we have included in this guide some examples of simple modifications.

EndNote has some other useful features like archiving graphic files (images, tables, and figures) and being able to insert them in a manuscript as if they were citations thus making captions, titles, numbering etc. much easier to handle.

A large collection of Manuscript Templates is incorporated in EndNote and these contain mainly settings to help the author to follow the author instructions including those that go far beyond the scope of reference handling.

The existence of EndNote with its collection of tools and devices does not reduce the author's responsibility to produce a final manuscript of the quality required to be fully compliant with prevailing instructions. Professional training, qualified user support and high quality literature are also key elements for success.

Finally, several recommended user settings have been included which sometimes are different from the default (factory) settings. These settings are experience based and will certainly save the beginner from many initial problems.

2. CHECKING YOUR INSTALLATION

A normal installation of EndNote provided Word is installed earlier will result in the following menu alternatives. Before you test the CWYW installation in Word exit from EndNote.

- Check Word: Go to **Tools - EndNote α**[1]:

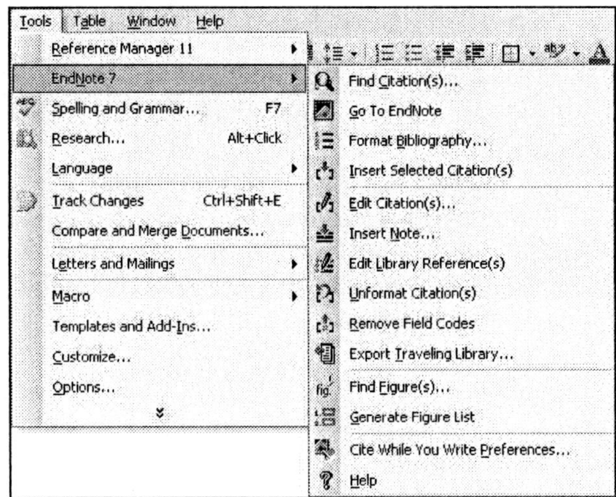

If these menu alternatives show then start EndNote from Word: Go to **Tools - EndNote α - Go to EndNote**.

- Check EndNote: Go to Tools -
  Cite While You Write [CWYW]:

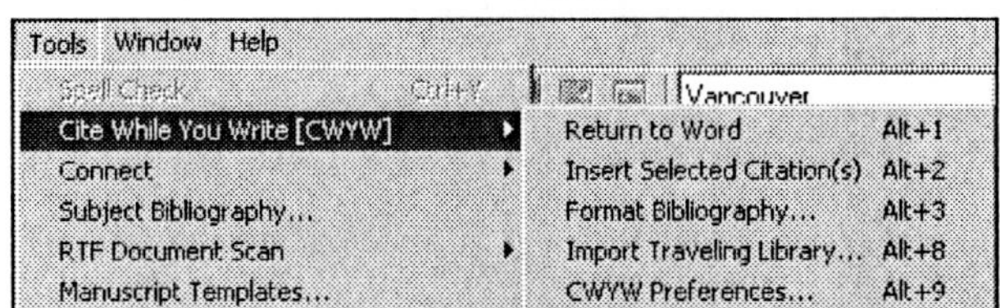

However, in many instances this particular part of the installation may not function immediately. The reason can be manifold, but one fairly common cause is that the originally defined Startup folder in Word has been deleted or moved after the installation of Word. Also when an update of Word takes place after EndNote has been installed then the CWYW menus could be lost.

[1] Where α represents 7, 8, 9, or 10 (X) depending on the EndNote-version.

The files that create the CWYW menus are:

For Word 97: EN7CWYW.wll
EN7CWYW.dot

For Word 2000: ENα[2]CWYW.wll
ENαCWYW.dot

For Word 2002, 2003: ENαCWYW.WordXP.wll
ENαCWYW.dot

These two respective files are installed in Word's so called Startup folder. The Startup folder is defined by the settings made when Word was first installed. The default startup folder is:
C:\Documents and Settings\<username>\Application Data\Microsoft\Word\STARTUP\

Note, when EndNote is installed and Word's default startup folder prevails, then the CWYW-files will be installed in the Startup folder belonging to the current username. This could be a problem when an Administrator logs in and installs EndNote on somebody's computer because when another user then logs in his Startup folder will be empty.

These settings may be verified or modified as follows:

♦ **Follow These Steps**

1 In Word go to **Tools** - **Options...**

2 Choose the **File Locations** tab.

3 Highlight the last line *Startup.*

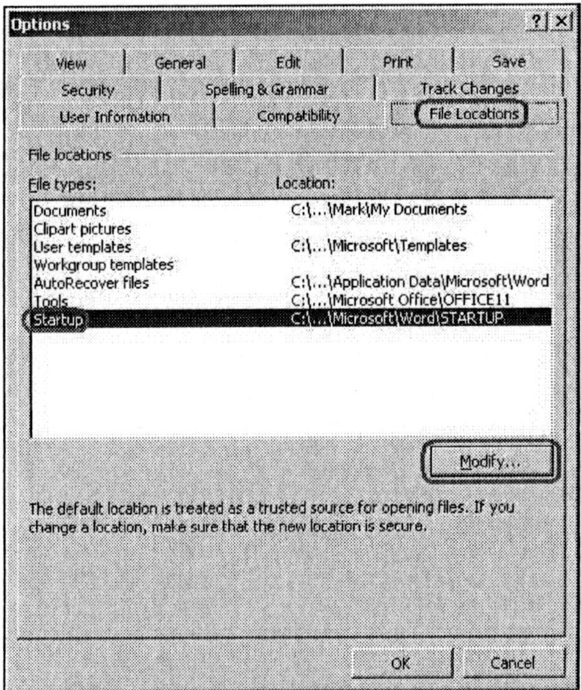

Provided the search path to the Startup folder is not hidden, you can use the [**Modify...**]-button and the drop-down list will clarify:

[2] Where α represents 7, 8, 9, or 10 (X) depending on the EndNote-version.

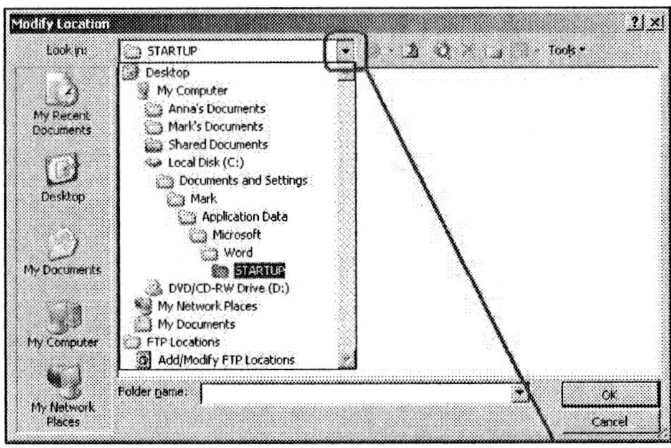

Once you know the complete search path to the Startup folder, use Windows Explorer to verify which files are actually residing there. Some of these folders may be hidden. To show hidden files and folders use Windows Explorer and go to **Tools - Folder Options...** and select the **View** tab:

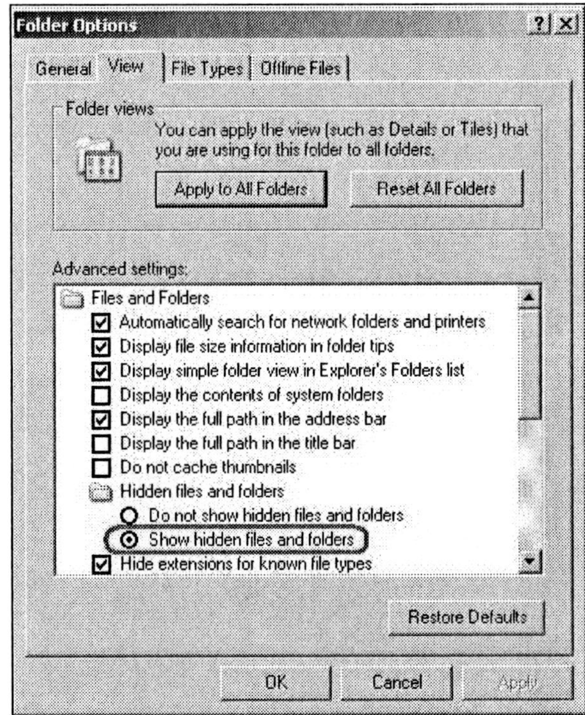

Check the option *Show hidden files and folders*, confirm with [**OK**]. You may now view the complete folder location of the Startup folder and inspect its contents:

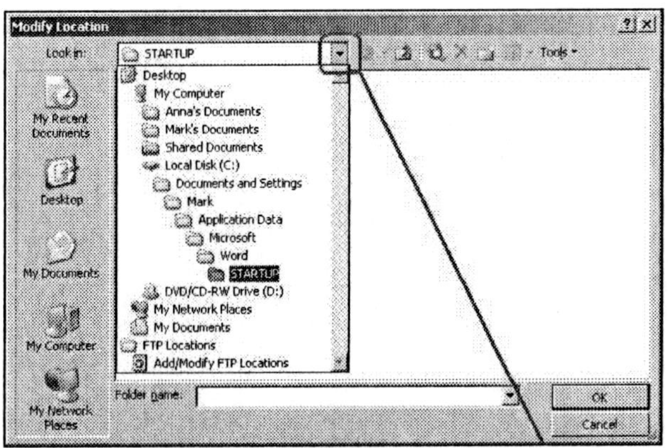

Sometimes this folder is empty or contains obsolete files. The EndNote installation folder contains archive copies of these files and EndNote is normally installed under C:\Program Files\EndNote\ or C:\Program Files\EndNote α[3]\. In case you cannot find the EndNote folder use instead the normal Search function in Windows to find the required files. When the files are properly copied in the current Startup folder you need to restart Word to activate the CWYW-functions.

Another way to verify proper installation is to use **Tools - Templates and Add-ins...** which will display the following dialog box:

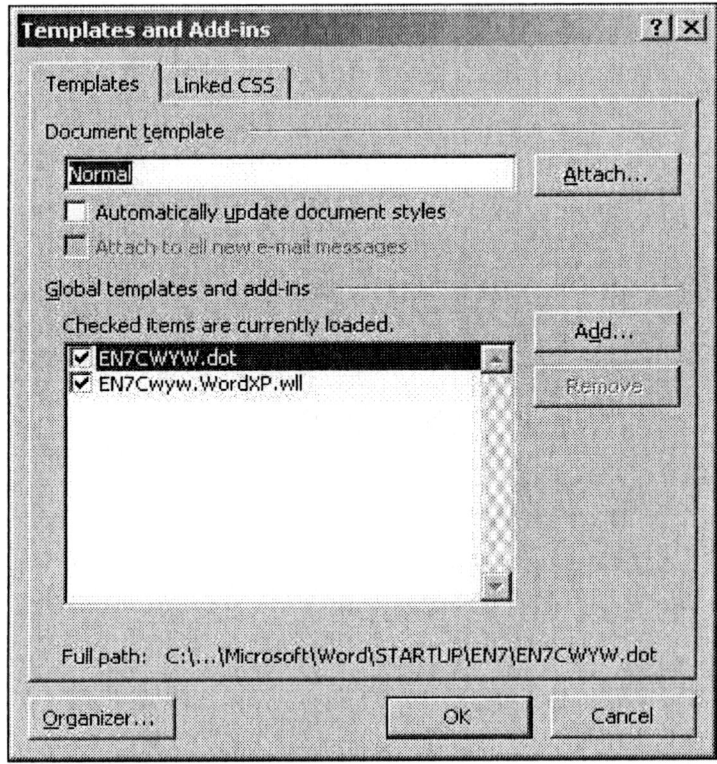

[3] Where α represents 7, 8, 9, or 10 (X) depending on the EndNote-version.

Sometimes it might be easier to create a new Startup folder and install the CWYW-files manually.

♦ **Follow These Steps**

1. Create a new folder called C:\Startup.
2. Copy
   EN7CWYW.dot *and* EN7CWYW.wll (Word 97)
   or
   ENα[4]CWYW.dot *and* ENαCWYW.wll (Word 2000)
   or
   ENαCWYW.dot *and* ENαCWYW.WordXP.wll (Word 2002, 2003)
   into this folder.
3. In Word go to **Tools** - **Options...**
4. Choose **File Locations** tab.
5. Highlight the last line *Startup.*
6. Use the [**Modify...**]-button to redefine the folder and confirm with the [**OK**]-button when C:\Startup has been selected.
7. Confirm with [**OK**] again.
8. Restart Word.

Updates and Patches

All software products and applications are continuously subject to modifications, updates, error corrections, and improvements. This section deals with updates and patches that are not new product versions but rather fixes that can be downloaded free-of-charge from the suppliers. EndNote has a menu alternative that verifies if your installation has the latest available update (not version) of the program.

Go to **Help - EndNote Program Updates...**

The connection will tell you if you have the latest update and if not, you can download directly from the program. Installing requires *Admin properties.* These updates can also add new content files (filters, connection files, styles) to your installation.

The latest updates available when this book went to print are:

- EndNote 7 no further update
- EndNote 8.0.2
- EndNote 9.0.1
- EndNote X

Your current program and update version can be verified by going to **Help - About EndNote.**

Word's patches are called Service Packs. EndNote is usually tested against the latest available Service Pack for Word. This implies that you may face performance disturbances for certain combinations of EndNote and Word. After having updated EndNote you might as well verify your current Word installation. See the following Microsoft sites for more information:

`http://office.microsoft.com/en-gb/officeupdate/default.aspx (U.K.)`

`http://office.microsoft.com/en-us/officeupdate/default.aspx (USA)`

[4] Where α represents 7, 8, 9, or 10 (X) depending on the EndNote-version.

3. IMPORTANT SETTINGS

This chapter deals with user settings in EndNote and Word. The settings are software specific and will have an impact on user simplicity, performance, and communication between them.

Toolbars in EndNote

Users may display or hide Toolbars. The settings are **Tools - Show Toolbar** and three options exist.

Tools - Show Toolbar - Main:

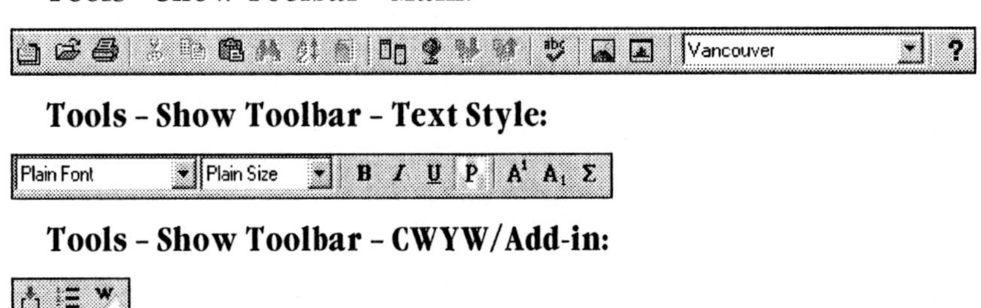

Tools - Show Toolbar - Text Style:

Tools - Show Toolbar - CWYW/Add-in:

General Preferences in EndNote

♦ **Follow These Steps**

1 From EndNote go to **Edit - Preferences...**

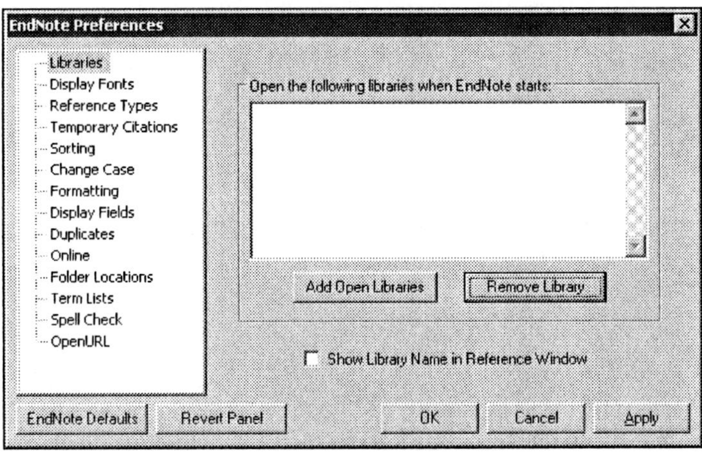

2 Select a section in the left hand box.

Only some of the listed sections will be commented on here, especially recommended settings that are different from the default (factory) settings.

Libraries: See comment on page 24.
Reference Types: See comment on page 28.
Temporary Citations: See comment on page 51.
Sorting: See comment on page 31.
Display Fields: See comment on page 30.
Duplicates: See comment on page 36.
Term Lists: See comment on page 91.
Spell Check: See comment on page 101.

CWYW Preferences

♦ **Follow These Steps**

From Word:

1 Go to **Tools - EndNote α**[5] **-**
Cite While You Write Preferences...
or key command **[Alt] + [9]**
or the icon .

From EndNote:

1 Go to **Tools - Cite While You Write [CWYW] -**
Cite While You Write Preferences...
or key command **[Alt] + [9]**.

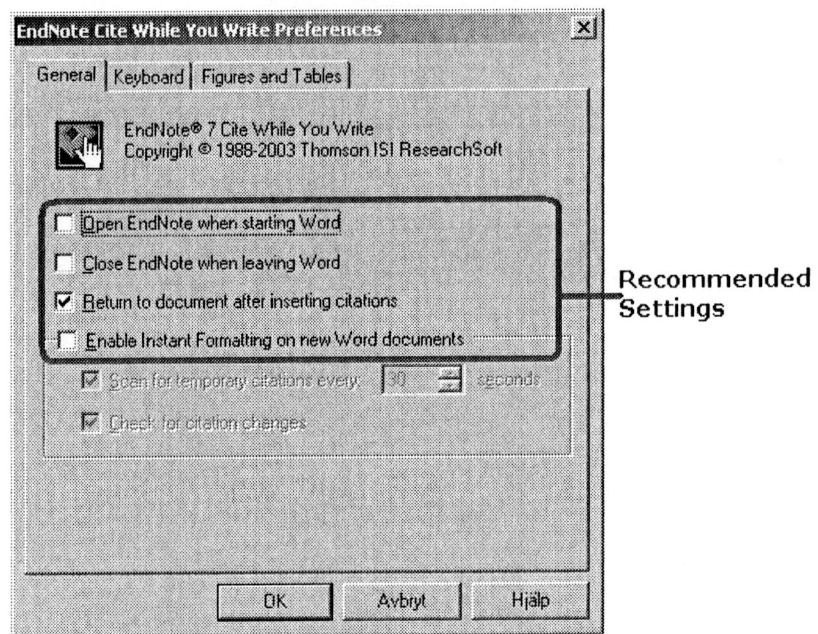

2 • *Uncheck* **Open EndNote When Starting Word,** *Recommended.*
• *Uncheck* **Close EndNote When Leaving Word**
• *Check* **Return to document after inserting citations,** *Recommended.*
• *Uncheck* **Enable Instant Formatting on new Word documents,** *Highly recommended. Note, this is the most important setting which will save you from many annoying disruptions in EndNote's performance!*

3 Confirm with **[OK]**.

[5] Where α represents 7, 8, 9, or 10 (X) depending on the EndNote-version.

Toolbar in Word

Users may display or hide the CWYW toolbar available from Word:
Go to **View** - **Toolbars** - **EndNote** α[6]:

The toolbar can be moved and a suitable location is at the top of the window near other toolbars.

Field Shading

In order to improve legibility during a work session it is suggested that the feature Field Shading be applied in Word.

- **Follow These Steps**
  1. Go to **Tools** - **Options...**
  2. Choose the **View** tab.
  3. Select **Field shading:** *Always* from the drop-down list.
  4. Confirm with **[OK]**.

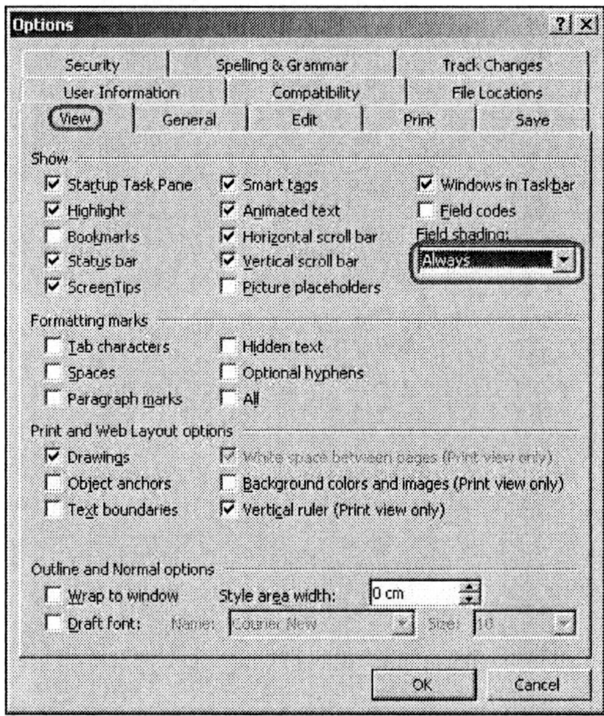

[6] Where α represents 7, 8, 9, or 10 (X) depending on the EndNote-version.

This setting results in citations and bibliographies created by EndNote being shaded:

Text·text·text·text·(1).·Text·text·text·text.·Text·text·text·text.·Text·text·text·text.·Text·text·text·text.·Te
text·text·text.·Text·text·text·text.·Text·text·text.·Text·text·text·text.·Text·text·text·text.·Text·text·text·te
(2).·Text·text·text·text.·Text·text·text·text.·Text·text·text·text.·Text·text·text·text.·Text·text·text·text.·
Text·text·text·text.·Text·text·text·text.·Text·text·text·text.·Text·text·text·text.·Text·text·text·text.·Text·
text·text·text.·Text·text·text·text·(3).¶

Bibliography¶

¶

1. → Yokoyama·A,·Kohno·N,·Sakai·K,·Hirasawa·Y,·Kondo·KaH.·Effect·of·pranlukast,·a·leukotriene·receptor·antagonist,·in·patients·with·severe·asthma·refractory·to·corticosteroids.·J·Asthma·1998;35(1):57-62.¶

2. → Vallerand·AH,·Riley-Doucet·C,·Hasenau·SM,·Templin·T.·Improving·cancer·pain·management·by·homecare·nurses.·Oncology·Nursing·Forum.·2004;31(4):809-16.¶

3. → Tischler·V,·Karim·K,·Rustall·S,·Gregory·P,·Vostanis·P.·A·family·support·service·for·homeless·children·and·parents:·users'·perspectives·and·characteristics.·Health·and·Social·Care·in·the·Community.·2004;12(4):327-35.¶

Field Codes

An EndNote formatted Word document contains embedded field codes the result of which is the citation(s) and the bibliography. However, Word has an option to allow field codes to be visible. Users do not normally need this option which is available from **Tools – Options...** and the **View** tab. When the option **Field codes** has been selected the result may be the following:

Text· {·ADDIN·EN.CITE·

<EndNote><Cite><Author>Zahn</Author><Year>2004</Year><RecNum>734</RecNum><MDL><REFERENCE_TYPE>0</REFERENCE_TYPE><REFNUM>734</REFNUM><AUTHORS><AUTHOR>Zahn,R.</AUTHOR><AUTHOR>Mark,B.</AUTHOR><AUTHOR>Niedermaier,N.</AUTHOR><AUTHOR>Zeymer,U.</AUTHOR><AUTHOR>Limbourg,P.</AUTHOR><AUTHOR>Ischinger,T.</AUTHOR><AUTHOR>Haerten,K.</AUTHOR><AUTHOR>Hauptmann,K.E.</AUTHOR><AUTHOR>Leitner,E.R.</AUTHOR><AUTHOR>Kasper,W.</AUTHOR><AUTHOR>Tebbe,U.</AUTHOR><AUTHOR>Senges,J.</AUTHOR></AUTHORS><YEAR>2004</YEAR><TITLE>Embolic·protection·devices·for·carotid·artery·stenting:·better·results·than·stenting·without·protection?</TITLE><VOLUME>25</VOLUME><NUMBER>17</NUMBER><PAGES>1550-1558</PAGES><DATE>2004/09//</DATE><ALTERNATE_TITLE>Eur.Heart·

Sometimes this option has been activated by mistake or by another user of the same computer. To switch off this option go to **Tools - Options...** and the **View** tab. Uncheck the option **Field codes**. Confirm with [**OK**].

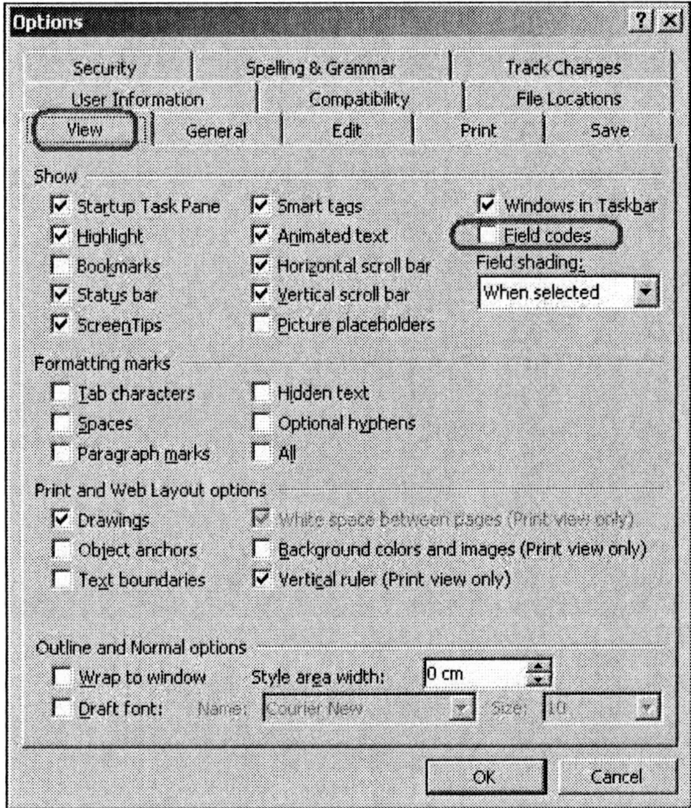

Spelling & Grammar

Word has Spelling and Grammar options which may be activated for automatic checking while writing. Depending on the native language selected for your document the result of automatic spelling and grammar checking may be as follows:

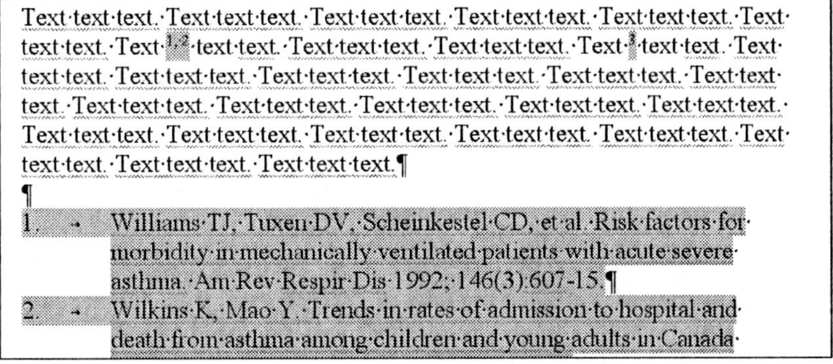

Text·text·text.·Text·text·text.·Text·text·text.·Text·text·text.·Text·text·text.·Text·text·text.·Text·[1,2]·text·text.·Text·text·text.·Text·text·text.·Text·[1]·text·text.·Text·text·text.·Text·text·text.·Text·text·text.·Text·text·text.·Text·text·text.·Text·text·text.·Text·text·text.·Text·text·text.·Text·text·text.·Text·text·text.·Text·text·text.·Text·text·text.·Text·text·text.·Text·text·text.·Text·text·text.·Text·text·text.·Text·text·text.·Text·text·text.¶

¶

1. → Williams·TJ,·Tuxen·DV,·Scheinkestel·CD,·et·al.·Risk·factors·for·morbidity·in·mechanically·ventilated·patients·with·acute·severe·asthma.·Am·Rev·Respir·Dis·1992;·146(3):607-15.¶
2. → Wilkins·K,·Mao·Y.·Trends·in·rates·of·admission·to·hospital·and·death·from·asthma·among·children·and·young·adults·in·Canada·

Words and terms identified by the spell or grammar checker are marked with a wavy line. Many users find this feature annoying during typing since almost all new authors and most scientific terms are identified by the spell checker. Another serious issue is that in many cases the spell and grammar checker disturbs the performance of Word and EndNote and sometimes even causes Word to crash.

In order to avoid such disruptions we suggest that automatic spell and grammar checkers are switched off. Go to **Tools - Options...** and the **Spelling & Grammar** tab. Uncheck **Check spelling as you type** and uncheck **Check grammar as you type**. Confirm with **[OK]**.

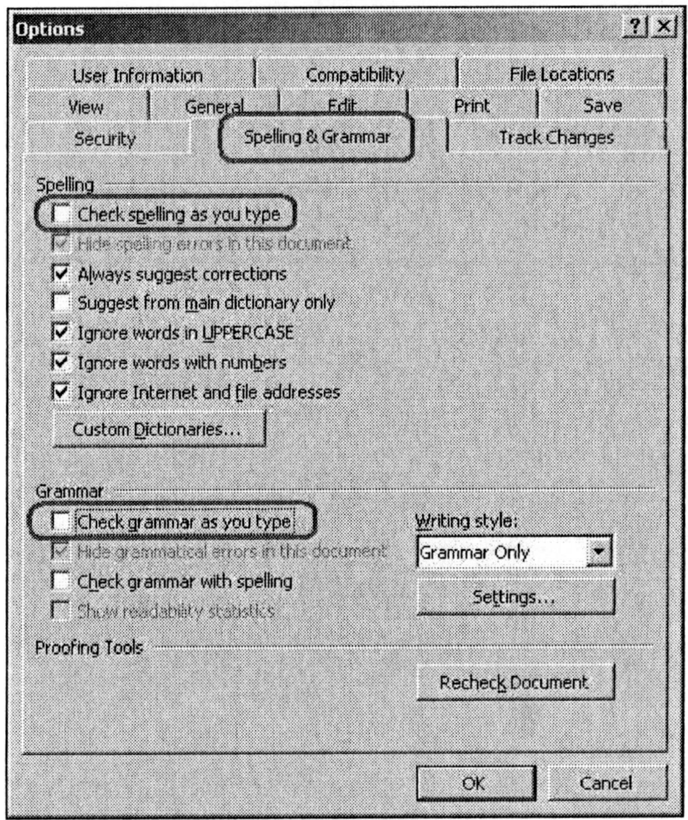

It is preferable that the spelling and grammar check is only carried out when the user so decides. The command is **Tools - Spelling and Grammar...** or key command **[F7]**.

Backup Copy, Fast Save

Word has an **Allow fast saves** option that only saves changes in the document. Such saving is faster but creates larger files than otherwise. Word also has a backup option that automatically saves the previous version of the document and with the file extension *.WBK. Using this latter option the Allow fast saves option is automatically disabled. We recommend the following setting. Go to **Tools - Options...** and the **Save** tab. Check the **Always create backup copy** option. Confirm with **[OK]**.

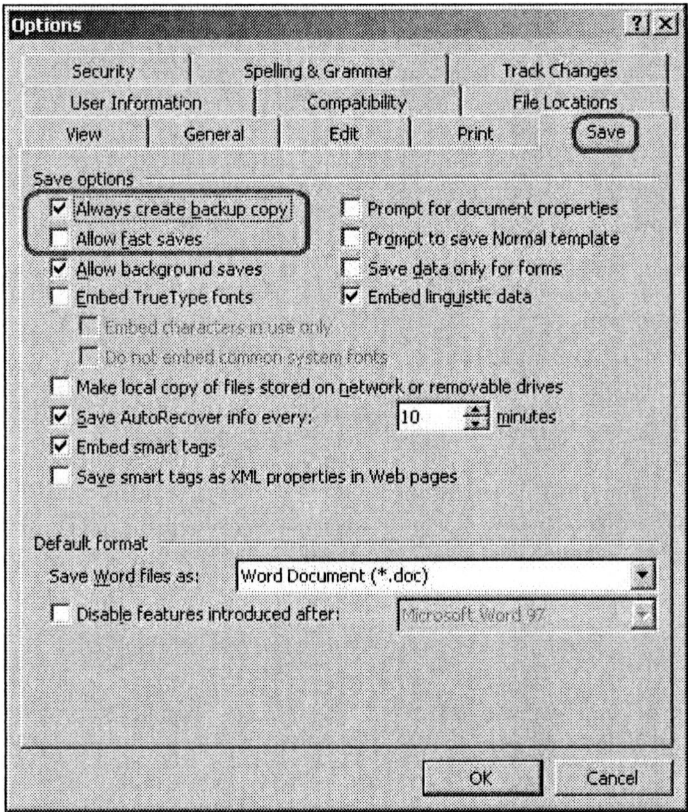

Startup of EndNote

EndNote can be started from Windows' startup menu:

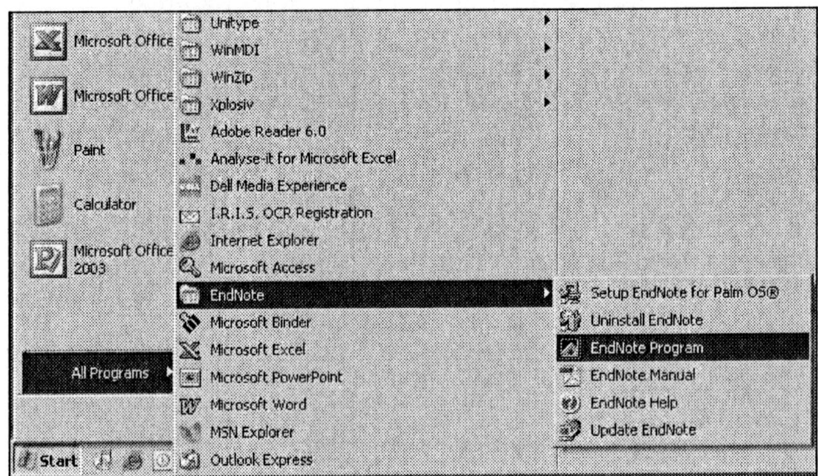

or from the shortcut icon .

When you start EndNote 'stand-alone' like this the CWYW-functions are *not* activated. The **Cite While You Write [CWYW]** is disabled under the **Tools** menu. The CWYW functions must be started from Word.

We also recommend the setting of a startup library from the **Edit - Preferences - Libraries**, see page 17, so that a certain library is automatically opened each time EndNote starts.

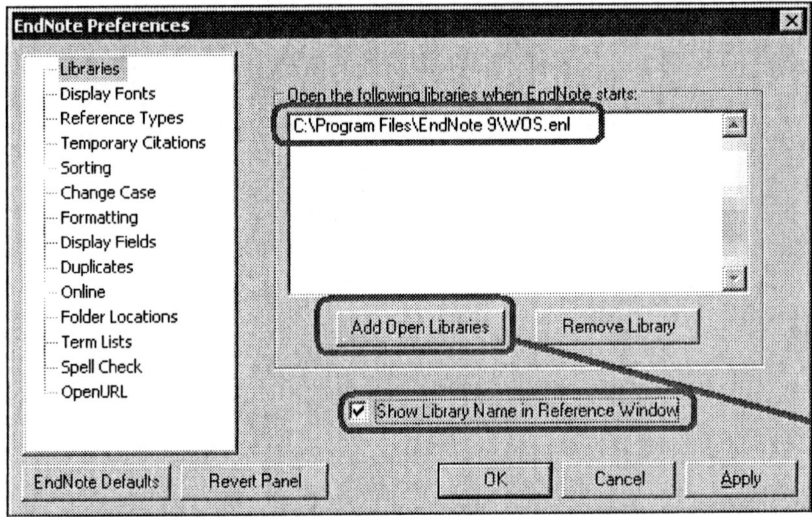

A practical and recommended startup procedure for Word and EndNote would therefore be:

♦ **Follow These Steps**

1. Start Word *before* EndNote. The CWYW-menu in Word is available even when EndNote is not started.
2. Start EndNote from Word with
   Tools - EndNote α[7] - Go To EndNote
   or key command **[Alt]** + **[1]**
   or the icon [icon].

With these recommendations EndNote will always start with active CWYW-functions and the current library opens automatically:

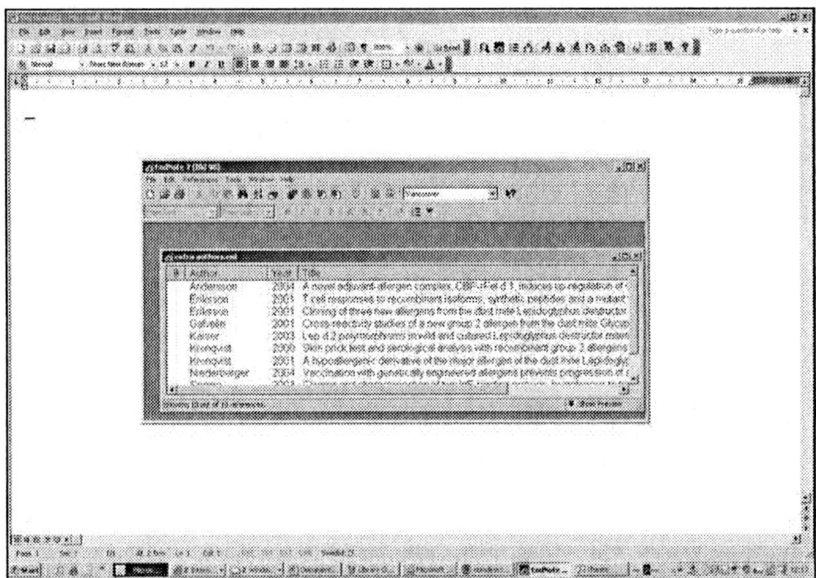

The Format Bibliography settings for a certain document, see page 53, including Style and layout, also prevails when the document is opened.

[7] Where α represents 7, 8, 9, or 10 (X) depending on the EndNote-version.

4. MANAGING LIBRARIES

An EndNote library is a uniform database with a certain number of records. Each record is a representation of a source of any kind, normally a book, a magazine, a book section, a journal article, a case, or statute or virtually any kind of literature which writers need to refer to.

Each record is built up of a certain number of fields and each field should contain a specific piece of information written and organized in a controlled way so that search and retrieval can be carried out reliably. A simple typing error could easily mean that an important record is not found when needed.

Each EndNote library is also a file with the file extension *.ENL which stands for EndNote Library.

Compatibility of Libraries

Libraries created by EndNote 7 or earlier have a limitation of 32 MB whereas EndNote 8 and later may have unlimited size. This implies that EndNote 7 libraries can be opened/converted by EndNote 8 or later but not vice versa. Such a conversion creates a new library and leaves the original library intact.

If you want to convert *backwards* from an EndNote 8 or later library to an EndNote 7 library then you need to export data using the output style *EndNote Export* and import data using the import option *EndNote Import* or the import filter *EndNote Import.enf*. The latter may need some modification in order to work satisfactorily because there are Reference Types and fields from EndNote 8 or later that do not exist in EndNote 7. See About Reference Types, page 28. Data will be transferred in the form of a normal textfile with the proprietary EndNote Tags or "%-tags".

See also Chapter 17, page 97, on exporting and importing data.

Creating New Libraries

♦ **Follow These Steps**

1. Create a new library with **File - New...**

   or the icon [icon].
2. Determine a folder location and a file name for the library.
3. Confirm with **[Save]**.

Where should one store the EndNote library? The EndNote library is as important for the user as any manuscript document. Care should be taken to ensure the backups are made of all your libraries. It is therefore recommended that libraries are stored along with their corresponding manuscripts in the same folder preferably on a server. Manual backups should be made for those documents and libraries stored solely on the hard drive of a PC.

Creating New Records

♦ **Follow These Steps**

1. Create a new record with **References - New Reference** or key command **[Alt]** + **[N]**
   or the icon
   or right-click the mouse and select **New Reference**.
2. Select applicable Reference Type from the drop-down list.
3. Type bibliographic or other data in the respective fields.
4. Save record with the close icon in the uppermost right corner of the Reference window.

In the case of a typing error in a new or existing record you may use the undo function **Edit - Undo** or **[Ctrl]** + **[Z]**. When a record is saved, which is the case as soon as it is closed, the undo function no longer works.

About Reference Types

EndNote 7 has 29 Reference Types and each reference type can have up to 40 fields. EndNote 8 and 9 have been increased to 38 Reference Types and 51 fields. EndNote X has been increased even further to 42 Reference Types. The default (factory) setting suggests certain specific Reference Types each with a subset of fields selected among the available fields. Reference Types and fields can be customized.

♦ **Follow These Steps**

1. Go to **Edit - Preferences**.
2. Choose the section **Reference Types**.
3. Click on **[Modify Reference Types]** and the following dialog box will appear:

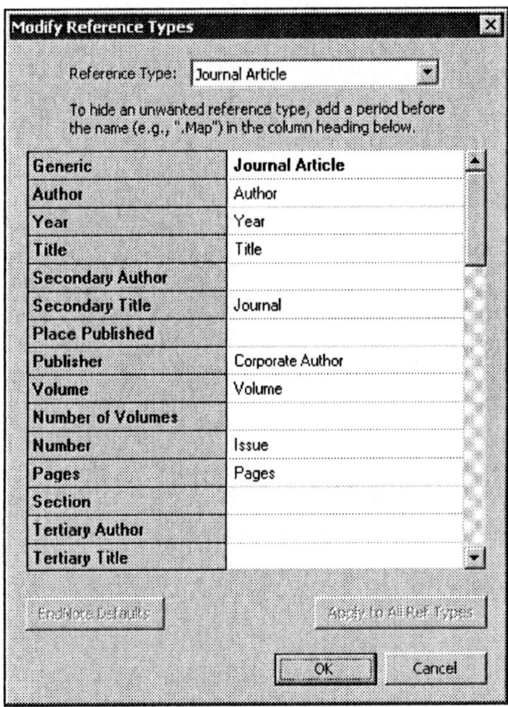

Reference Type Generic uses all fields and default field names but all other Reference Types can be edited by the user. Deletion of a field name implies that the field is not used. The dropdown list beside **Reference Type:** offers you options for editing each Reference Types separately. The sorting order for Reference Types is alphabetic for EndNote X or later. This implies that modifying the Reference Type name reorders the dropdown list. **[EndNote Defaults]** and **[Apply to All Ref Types]** are only active when you start editing already saved settings.

If you need to hide a certain Reference Type then type a full stop before the name, for example "`.Patent`".

4 Save modified settings with **[OK]**.

The settings for Reference Types and fields are saved in Windows Registry for EndNote 8 or earlier whereas EndNote 9 or later stores these settings in a separate file, *RefTypeTable.xml*, located in C:\Document and Settings\<user name>\Application Data\EndNote\. This will simplify the reproduction of customized settings of Reference Types between users.

About Record Numbers

EndNote dedicates a unique Record Number for each new record added to a library starting with #1. Record numbers cannot be edited by the user. A *deleted record cannot be replaced* by a new record with the same record number. Record numbers are used in Word documents as the internal address from a citation to a record of a certain library.

About Author and Other Personal Names

The following generic fields are reserved for personal names: Author, Secondary Author, Tertiary Author, and Subsidiary Author. Names in these fields must follow certain conventions. Basic rule is that each name must be typed on a *separate line*. The following variations are accepted:

```
Pettersson, T.G.
Pettersson, TG
Tage G. Petterson
Tage G Petterson
Tage Petterson
van Beethoven, Ludwig
von Euler, F
de la Gardie, Magnus
```

Whenever a name prefix is used like in **`von Euler`**, the rule is *Surname, First name.*

The comma is essential. If a comma is omitted then EndNote will always interpret the last word as Secondary name.

Displaying Fields and Sorting a Library

An open library may have the following appearance:

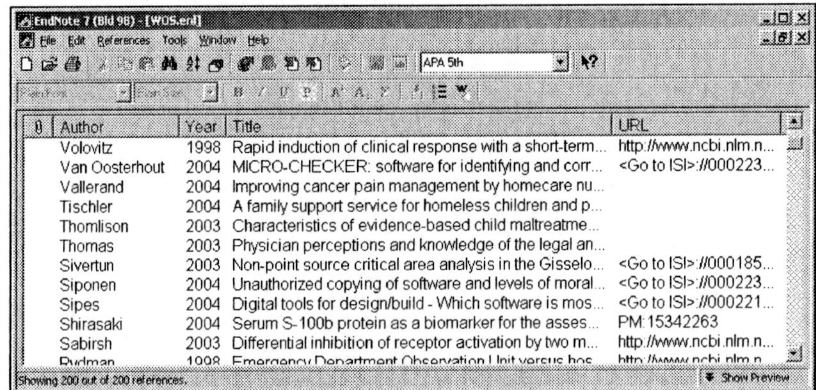

Each record is one line in the library window. The fields displayed in the library window are determined by settings in EndNote.

♦ **Follow These Steps**

1. Go to **Edit - Preferences.**
2. Choose the section **Display Fields** and the following dialog box will appear:

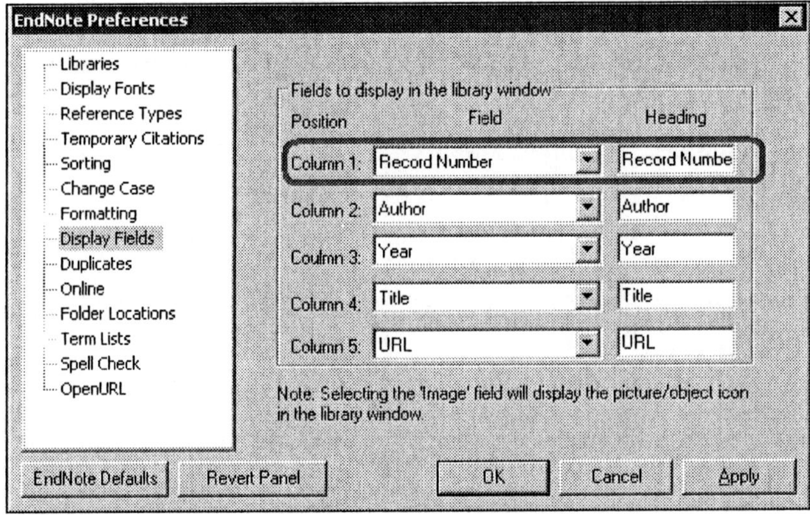

EndNote 9 or earlier can display 5 columns in the library window whereas EndNote X has been extended to display up to 8 columns.

The Image field will display a clip symbol in the library window for references with a file attachment and the Link to PDF field will display a PDF icon (only for EndNote X).

Many users prefer to display the records numbers in the library window. The drop-down list for **Column 1** can be used to select Record Number.

The result after confirming this modification with **[OK]** is:

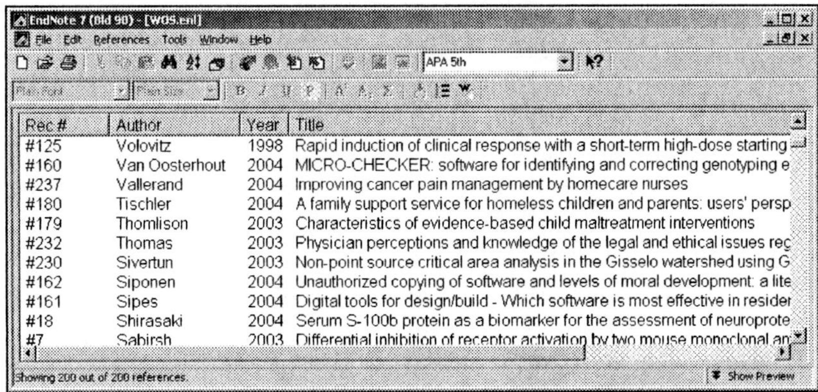

A library can be sorted according to various sorting options under **References - Sort References....** It is also convenient to simply use the column heads in the library window. A click on the column head **Rec #** will display the following sorting:

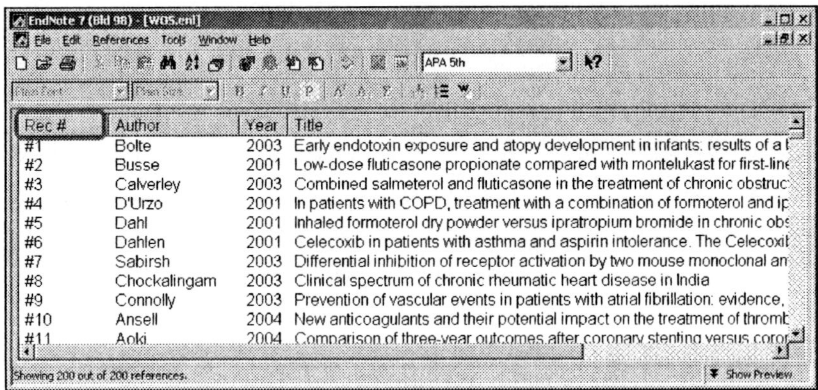

Another click on the same column head will reverse the sort order. The sorting principles can be modified so that various common prepositions to family names like van, von, de la or short words in a title (like 'a', 'an', 'the') are neglected when sorting. Such modifications can be made under **Edit - Preferences - Sorting**, see page 17.

Copying, Cutting, and Pasting References

An EndNote user can organize references in many ways. Some users prefer to create one large master library for multiple uses whereas others prefer several libraries. Whatever principle one adopts, there will certainly be a need for transfer record(s) from one library to another. Some use temporary libraries and examine the records before they are transferred to their final library.

Highlight a record with the pointer and a click. If you need to highlight more than one record hold the **[Ctrl]**-key while selecting. An interval of records is selected by holding the **[Shift]**-key while highlighting the first and the last record. Finally, all records are selected with **Edit - Select All** or key command **[Ctrl] + [A]**.

Cutting record(s):

♦ **Follow These Steps**

1 Activate the current "from" Library.
2 Highlight one or several records.
3 Go to **Edit - Cut**
or key command **[Ctrl] + [X]**
or the icon
or right-click the mouse and select **Cut**.

Copying record(s):

♦ **Follow These Steps**

1 Activate the current "from" Library.
2 Highlight one or several records.
3 Go to **Edit - Copy**
or key command **[Ctrl] + [C]**
or the icon
or right-click the mouse and select **Copy**.

Pasting record(s):

♦ **Follow These Steps**

1 Activate the current "to" Library.
2 Go to **Edit - Paste**
or key command **[Ctrl] + [V]**
or the icon
or right-click the mouse and select **Paste**.

Drag and drop equals a Copy/Paste procedure.

Pasting a record means that an exact copy of all information in all fields are copied into the new library. One important remark however, is that the record number is determined by the new library. Each library has its own individual record numbering.

Copying a Library - Save a Copy

Neither an EndNote library nor an open record has access to the Save or Save As commands. These commands are instead available for other functions in the program such as editing of filters, connection files, or styles.

A library is saved as soon as all its records are saved which takes place as soon as a new or modified record is closed.

Therefore EndNote has a proprietary command which is activated when a library is open and all its records are closed.

The command is:

File - Save a Copy...

Then the file location and file name need to be determined.

The copy created with this command is an exact copy including the record numbering (even with missing record numbers) and with the complete attachment folder as mentioned on page 45.

Copying a Library – Saving a Compressed Copy of a Library

EndNote X offers a new method of saving a Library and the attachment folder and all its contents as one zipped file with file extension *.enlx.

♦ **Follow These Steps**

1. Open the Library that you want to compress.
2. Go to **File - Send To - Compressed Library...**
3. Determine name and allocation of the new compressed library.
4. Confirm with **[Save]**.

Decompressing is made by the normal **File - Open - Open Library...** command or key command **[Ctrl] + [O]**.

Merging Libraries

There are two methods at hand to merge two libraries into one.

For relatively small libraries we recommend:

♦ **Follow These Steps**

1. Activate the current "from" Library.
2. Highlight all records with **Edit - Select All** or key command **[Ctrl] + [A]**.
3. Go to **Edit - Copy** or key command **[Ctrl] + [C]** or the icon or right-click the mouse and select **Copy**.
4. Activate the "to" library.
5. Go to **Edit - Paste** or key command **[Ctrl] + [V]** or the icon or right-click the mouse and select **Paste**.

For relatively large libraries we recommend:

♦ **Follow These Steps**

1. Activate the current "to" Library.
2. Go to **File - Import...**

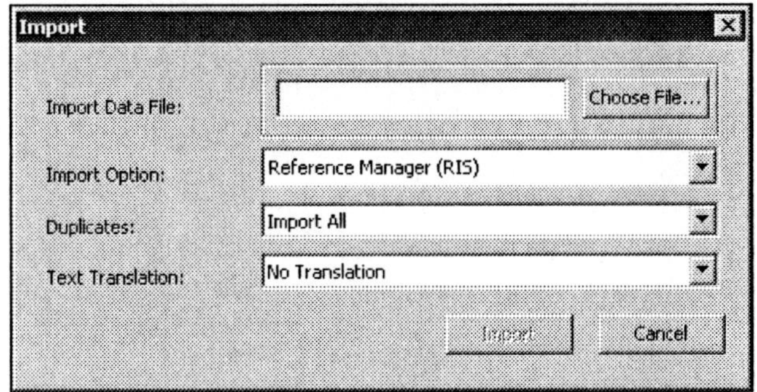

3. Use **[Choose File]** to browse until you find the "from" library. When the "from" library has been selected the Import Option is automatically set as EndNote Library.

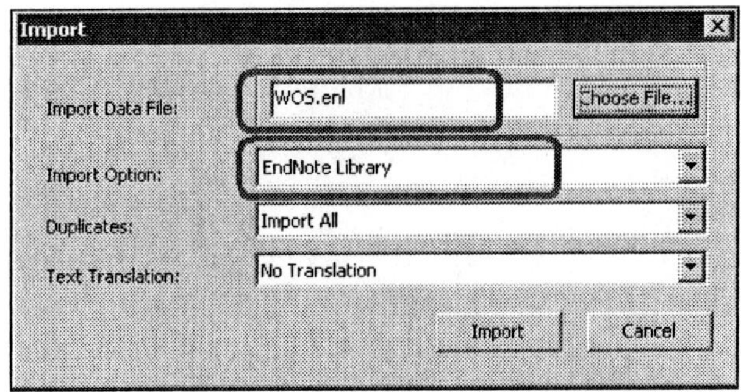

4 Import with the **[Import]**-button.
5 Show all references in the "merged" library with **References - Show All References** or key command **[Ctrl]** + **[M]** or right-click the mouse and select **Show All References**.

Searching References

- **Follow These Steps**

1 Activate the current library.
2 Go to **References - Search References...** or key command **[Ctrl]** + **[F]** or the icon or right-click the mouse and select **Search References...**

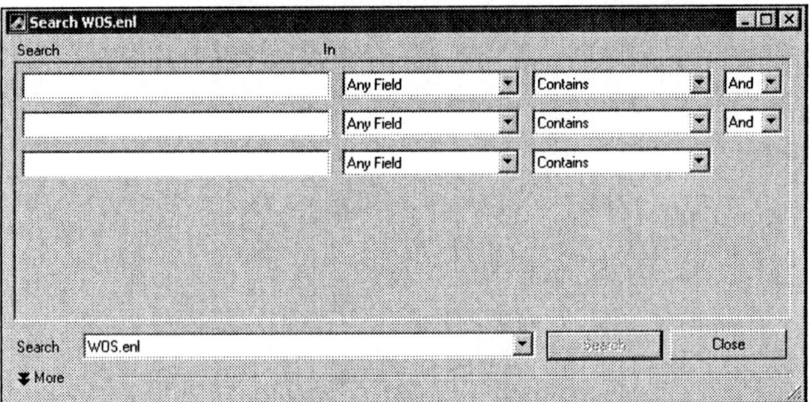

3 Type search word(s) and select fields with the drop-down list. Operators And, Or, or Not are also selected with the drop-down lists.

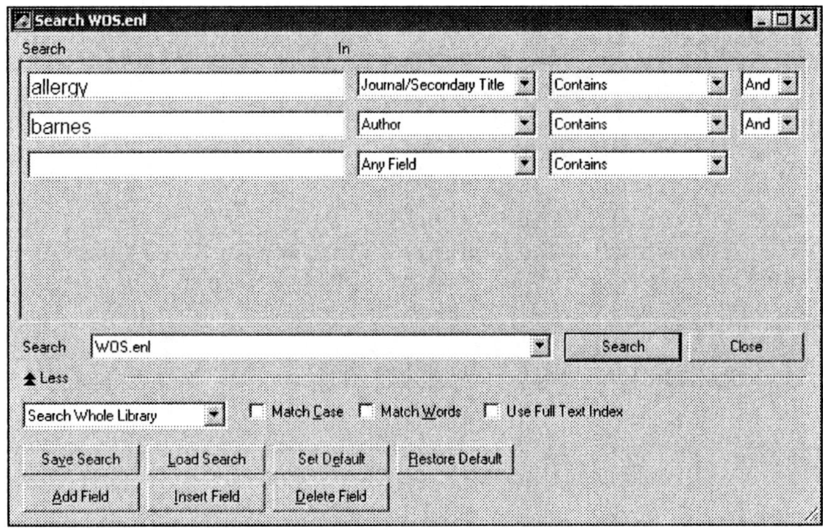

4 Search with the **[Search]**-button.

The result of the search is the library window with all but the found record(s) hidden:

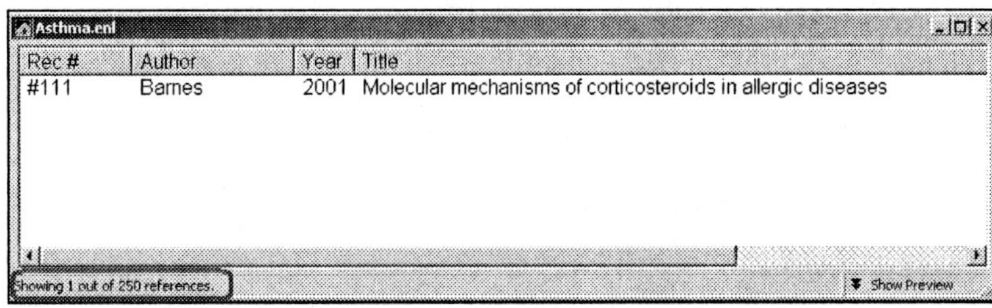

When you need to display all records again, go to **References - Show All References...** or key command **[Ctrl]** + **[M]** or right-click the mouse and select **Show All References...**

Useful settings (use the **More**-button) in the search form are:

Resizing by means of dragging with the pointer in one side or in one corner

[Save Search]: Saving a complete search expression.

[Load Search]: Loading of saved search expressions.

[Set Default]: Stores resizing, number of text boxes, specific fields in the drop-down list, and operators.

[Restore Default]: Always restores the current default settings of the search form with *blank text boxes.*

[Add Field]: Will add a new text box for more complex search expressions.

[Insert Field]: Will add a new text box above the current position of the cursor.

[Delete Field]: Deletes the text box of the current position of the cursor.

Deleting References

♦ **Follow These Steps**

1 Highlight the reference(s) you need to delete.
2 Go to **Edit - Clear**
or **References - Delete References...**
or key command **[Ctrl]** + **[D]**
or right-click the mouse and select **Delete References...**

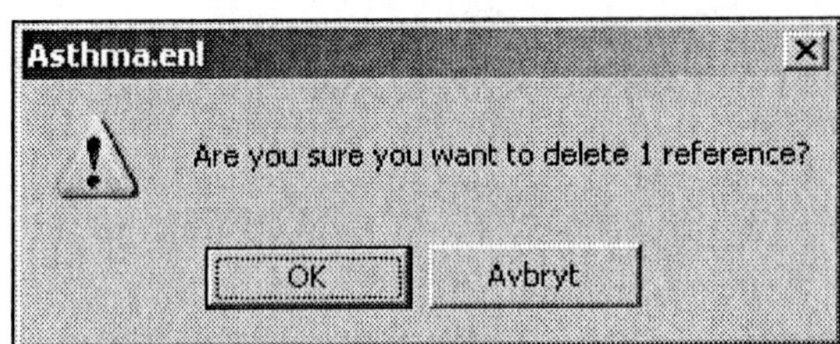

3 Confirm with **[OK]**.

Finding Duplicates

Duplicate search criteria are based on settings made under **Edit - Preferences - Duplicates**, see page 17.

♦ **Follow These Steps**

1 Activate current library.
2 Go to **References - Find Duplicates**.

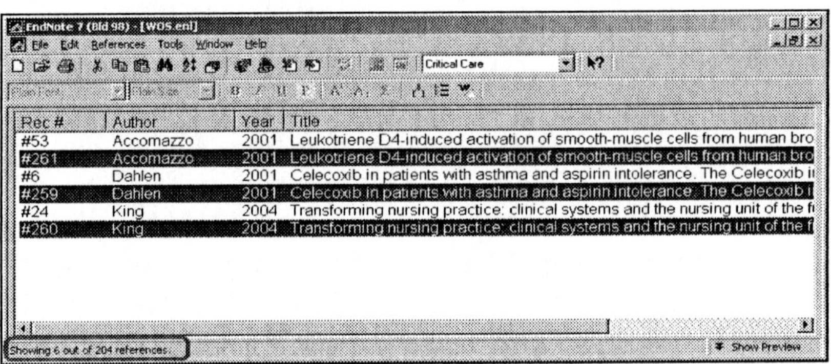

These duplicates found are displayed so that all records other than those with the lowest record numbers in each set are highlighted. Highlighted records may now be deleted.

Opening Records and Browsing a Library

♦ **Follow These Steps**

1 Activate current library.
2 Highlight *one* reference and apply
References - Edit References
or key command **[Ctrl]** + **[E]**
or right-click the mouse and select **Edit References**
or **[Enter]**
or double-click the selected reference.

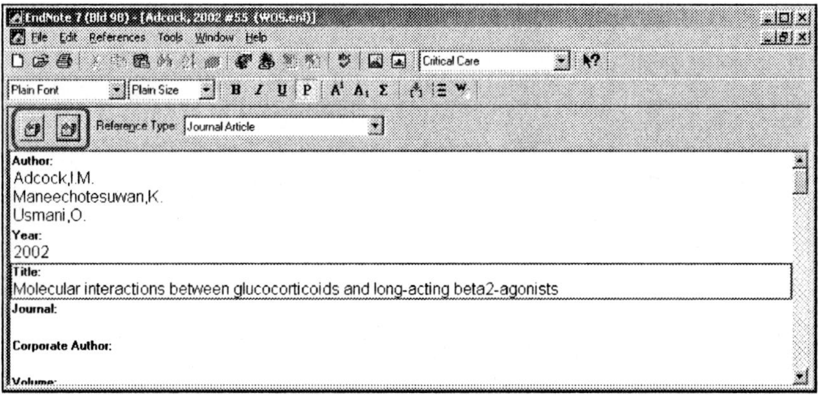

3 Browse records in the current sort order with the browse buttons in the leftmost upper corner of the record window
or **References - Next Reference**
or **[Ctrl]** + **[PgDn]**
alternatively
References - Previous Reference
or **[Ctrl]** + **[PgUp]**.

The Author field is by default selected as the current field indicated by a frame each time a record is opened. However, any other field can be selected which makes field browsing possible: The current field[8] of each record will be displayed when browsing records. Please note, that the current field indicated by the frame is also the normal edit mode for a field.

A practical feature has been introduced in EndNote X, the option to hide empty fields. In the Reference window, upper rightmost corner is a button that toggles between **Hide Empty Fields** and **Show Empty Fields**:

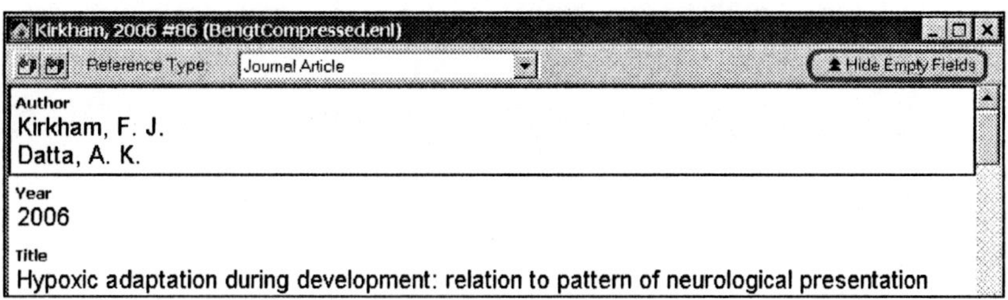

[8] Due to imperfections in EndNote 8 the the current field is not displayed automatically when browsing.

5. INSERTING CITATIONS

First decide where in the text of the Word document the citation should be located. The position is determined by the cursor.

Then decide which reference(s) from the EndNote library should be inserted. The choice is confirmed by highlighting those references.

♦ **Follow These Steps**

1. Place the cursor on the location of the citation (Word).
2. Go to EndNote with
   Tools - EndNote α[9] - Go To EndNote
   or key command **[Alt]** + **[1]**
   or the icon .
3. Highlight the reference(s) to be inserted. If you need to highlight more than one reference hold the **[Ctrl]**-key while selecting. A continuous interval of references is highlighted when you hold the **[Shift]**-key while highlighting the first and the last references of the interval.
4. The insertion command is made either from Word or from EndNote.
   From EndNote:
   Tools - Cite While You Write [CWYW] - Insert Citation(s)
   or key command **[Alt]** + **[2]**
   or the icon .
   After insertion you will return automatically to Word if the settings suggested on page 18 have been applied.
   From Word:
   Tools - EndNote α - Insert Citation(s)
   or key command **[Alt]** + **[2]**
   or the icon .

In case you will need to return to Word from EndNote at any occasion the following alternatives are at hand:

- **Tools - Cite While You Write [CWYW] - Return to Word**
- Key command **[Alt]** + **[1]**
- Use the icon
- Windows standard program switch, **[Alt]** + **[Tab]**
- Use the program buttons of the program bar in Windows:

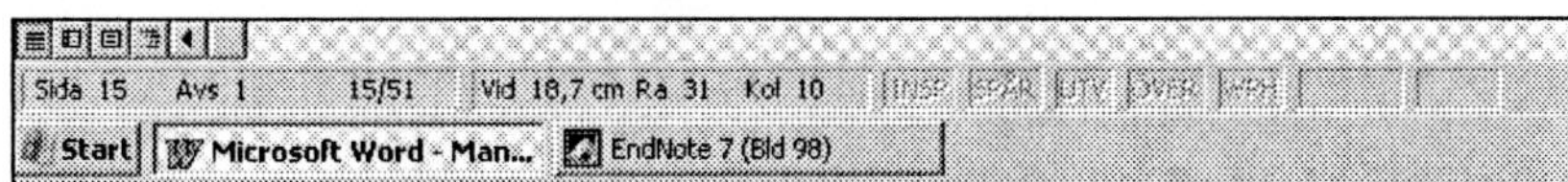

Our conclusion is that the easiest way to toggle between Word and EndNote is with key command **[Alt]** + **[1]** which works from either program.

[9] Where α represents 7, 8, 9, or X depending on the EndNote-version.

Other alternatives for insertion of citations are:

- Copy reference(s) from EndNote with **[Ctrl]** + **[C]** and paste into Word with **[Ctrl]** + **[V]**.
- Right-click and select **Copy** from EndNote and **Paste** into Word.
- Drag and drop from EndNote to Word.
- From Word:
  Tools - **EndNote α[10]** - **Find Citation(s)...**
  or key command **[Alt]** + **[7]**
  or the icon .

Then use the new Search window to search for your references, highlight, and apply with the **[Insert]**-button:

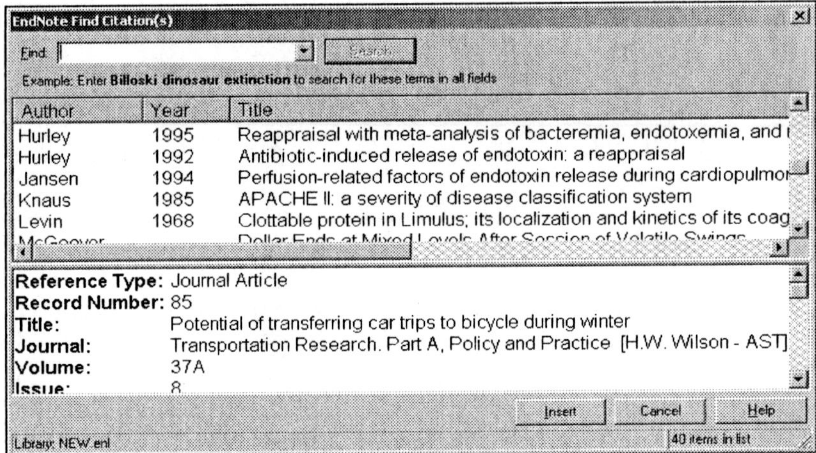

The result of insertion of citation(s) is:

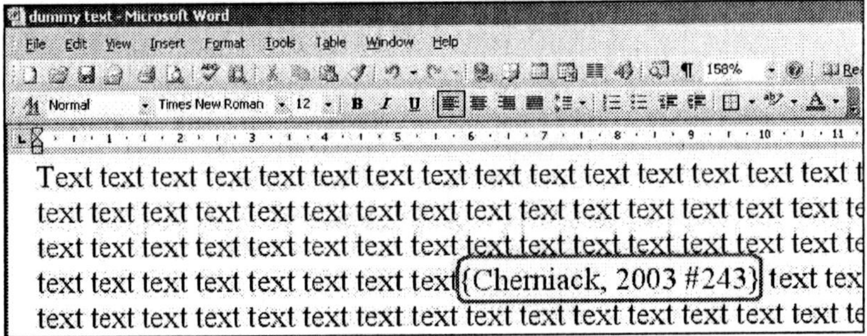

This is the typical *Temporary Citation*:
`{Cherniack, 2003 #243}` or if two references are inserted
`{Cherniack, 2003 #243;Patel, 2004 #472}`
The surrounding curly bracket, `{.. .}` is called the *Temporary Citation Delimiter* and **#243** is the record number mentioned earlier.

Please note, that if the suggested settings from page 18 (Enable Instant Formatting ..) have not been applied then the program will instantly format a bibliography using the current Style.

See Chapter 9, page 51 on how to format the bibliography.

[10] Where α represents 7, 8, 9, or X depending on the EndNote-version.

6. INSERTING FOOTNOTES

Again first decide where in the text of the Word document the footnote with the citation should be inserted. The position of the footnote is determined by the cursor. Word's standard footnote feature is then used.

Then decide which reference(s) from the EndNote library should be inserted. The choice is confirmed by highlighting the selected reference(s).

- **Follow These Steps**
  1. In Word place the cursor on the location of the footnote.
  2. Go to **Insert - Footnotes and EndNotes...**
     or key command **[Ctrl]** + **[Alt]** + **[F]**.

The footnote window will open (normal layout) as shown below:

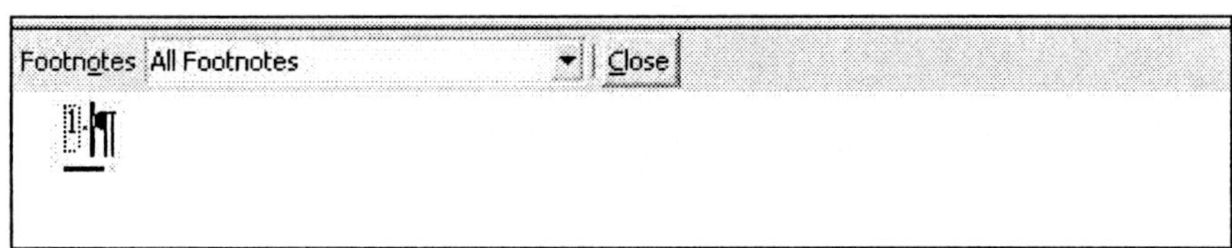

The insertion position of the citation in the footnote window will then be determined.

3. Go to EndNote with
   Tools - EndNote α[11] **- Go To EndNote**
   or key command **[Alt]** + **[1]**
   or the icon .
4. Highlight the reference(s) to be inserted. If you need to highlight more than one reference hold the **[Ctrl]**-button while selecting. A continuous interval of references is highlighted when you hold the **[Shift]**-key while highlighting the first and the last references of the interval.
5. The insertion command is made either from Word or from EndNote.
   From EndNote:
   Tools - Cite While You Write [CWYW] - Insert Citation(s)
   or key command **[Alt]** + **[2]**
   or the icon .
   After inserting you will return automatically to Word when the setting suggested on page 18 has been applied.
   From Word:
   Tools - EndNote α - Insert Citation(s)
   or key command **[Alt]** + **[2]**
   or the icon .

[11] Where α represents 7, 8, 9, or X depending on the EndNote-version.

Regarding the toggle between Word and EndNote and other alternative commands for insertion of references, please refer to previous section.

The result of this command, with three footnotes, is the following:

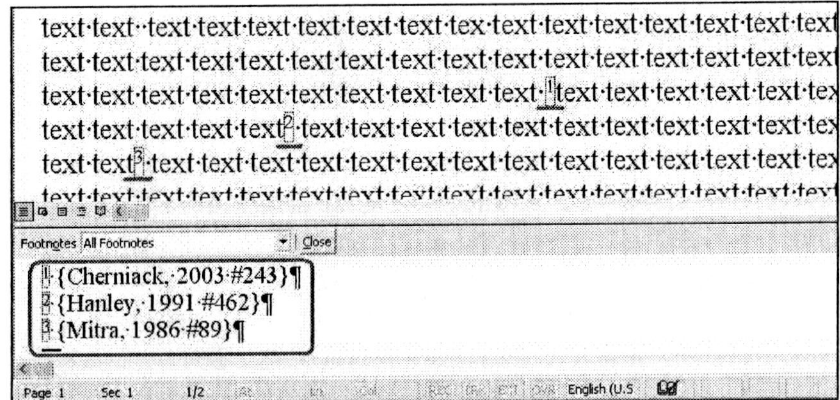

This again is the typical *Temporary Citation*:

{Cherniack, 2003 #243}

The surrounding curly bracket, **{.. .}** is called the *Temporary Citation Delimiter* and **#243** is the record number as has been mentioned earlier.

About footnote settings in Styles, see page 83.

For formatting the bibliography, see Chapter 9, page 51.

7. INSERTING GRAPHS AND IMAGES

EndNote offers the option to archive graphic files (images, tables, figures) as records in an EndNote Library. Virtually any type of file format may be used as an attachment of such EndNote record, but this section deals with graphic files only. Once residing as an attachment of a record the graphics may be used similarly as any bibliographic record that can be inserted, formatted, edited and labeled in a Word manuscript. Each record can only store *one* graphics file and the field used for the attachment is the generic field *Image* which must be activated for the Reference Type in question. By default all reference types use the Image field. The field *Caption* is reserved for the label which will be displayed together with the graph in a Word manuscript.

Three reference types have been especially dedicated for storing such graphic files: Figure, Chart or Table, and Equation. However, any reference type may store a graphics file or any other file.

Reference Type *Figure* will create a listing of Figures with the in-text citation (Figure 1), (Figure 2), (Figure 3) etc. and the text **List of Figures** when the output style has been set to create a list of figures at the end of the document.

All other reference types will create in-text citations (Table 1), (Table 2), (Table 3), etc and the text **List of Tables** when the output style has been set to create a list of tables at the end of the document.

Creating a Record with a Graphics Attachment

First we need to create an EndNote record with a graphics file.

♦ **Follow These Steps**

1 Create a new reference with **References - New Reference** or key command **[Alt] + [N]**
or the icon
or right-click the mouse and select **New Reference**.

2 Select Reference Type *Figure* from the drop-down list.

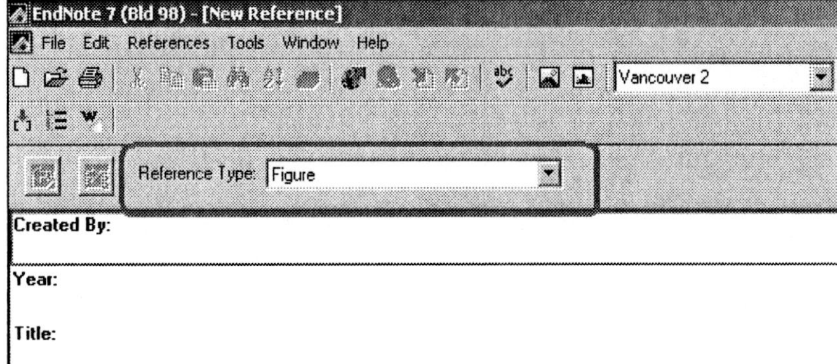

3 Go to **References - Insert Picture...**
   or the icon
4 Browse through folders and files until you have selected the graphics file that you want to use.
5 Confirm with **[Open]**.
6 Type applicable text in the other fields of the EndNote record especially in the Caption field because this text will be displayed together with the graph in the Word manuscript.

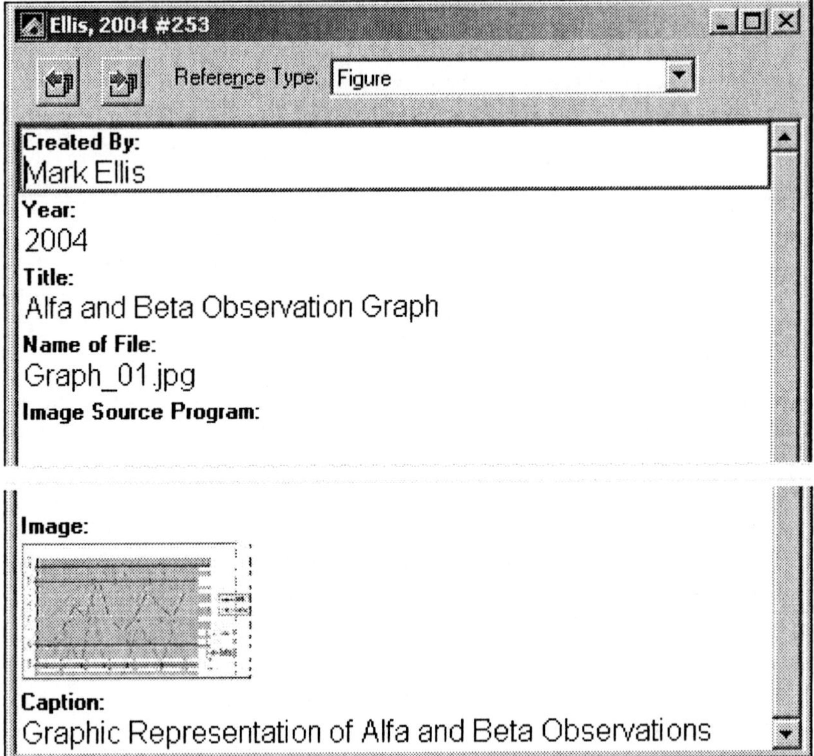

The graph is represented by a thumbnail or an icon in the Image field. By clicking on the thumbnail or the icon the associated application opens allowing editing to take place.

Each record can only store *one* graphics file. If you need to replace the file then the command **References - Insert Picture...** inserts the new file and the previous is replaced. If you need to delete a file then mark the Image field of a record and apply the **[Delete]**-key.

The new data in the record is saved when the Reference window is closed.

Where is the Attachment stored?

During the described procedure the following takes place. The inserted file is *copied* and stored in a folder named [Library].DATA[12]. This folder is created under the folder where the library is residing.

Example: The current Library is MedLab.enl and resides in the folder ..\Libraries\ i.e. ..\ Libraries\MedLab.enl

The command **Insert Picture...** creates a copy of the file, Graph_01.jpg, which is located on our computer or located on a server in our local network.

The copy is called:
..\Libraries\MedLab.DATA\nnnnnnnnnnGraph_01.jpg
The nnnnnnnnnn represents an arbitrary ten digit prefix to the original file name. Each record creates an individual attachment and if two records should insert same graphics file one copy for each record is then created. When an attached graphics file is deleted from the Image-field with the **[Del]**-key then the source (the copy of the file) is also deleted.

When the command **File - Save a Copy...** is applied, then the program automatically creates not only a copy of the current library but also an attachment folder including all graphics or other attachments. An alternative for EndNote X or later, Saving a Compressed Copy, is described on page 33.

Also, when you need to merge libraries either by means of copying and pasting records or by means of importing one library into another, see page 33, Merging Libraries, then the attachment(s) will be automatically copied into the attachment folder of the target library.

When moving or copying an EndNote library by means of Windows Explorer, however, you must then remember to also copy the folder containing the attachments.

Finally, exporting records from a library according to page 97 does not allow for the inclusion of any attachments, only the text contents of any field are included in the current style.

Inserting Graphs and Images in a Word Manuscript

The position of the in-text citation of a table or figure is determined by the position of the cursor. All operations are made from Word.

♦ **Follow These Steps**

1 Position the cursor in the Word document.

2 Go to **Tools - EndNote α[13] - Find Figures...**

or the icon [fig.]. Then the following dialog box appears:

[12] EndNote 8 or higher creates this folder (empty) as soon as a new library is created.

[13] Where α represents 7, 8, 9, or X depending on the EndNote-version.

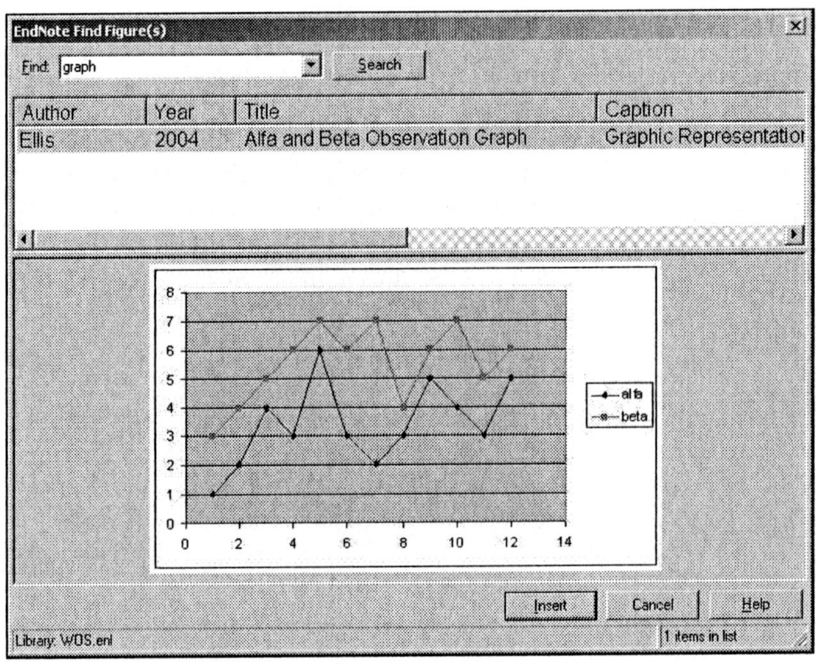

3 Type a search word in the **Find:** box then apply [**Search**]. Such search is automatically limited to records with an Image attachment.

4 When the desired record shows then highlight the record and apply the [**Insert**]-button.

The result may be like this:

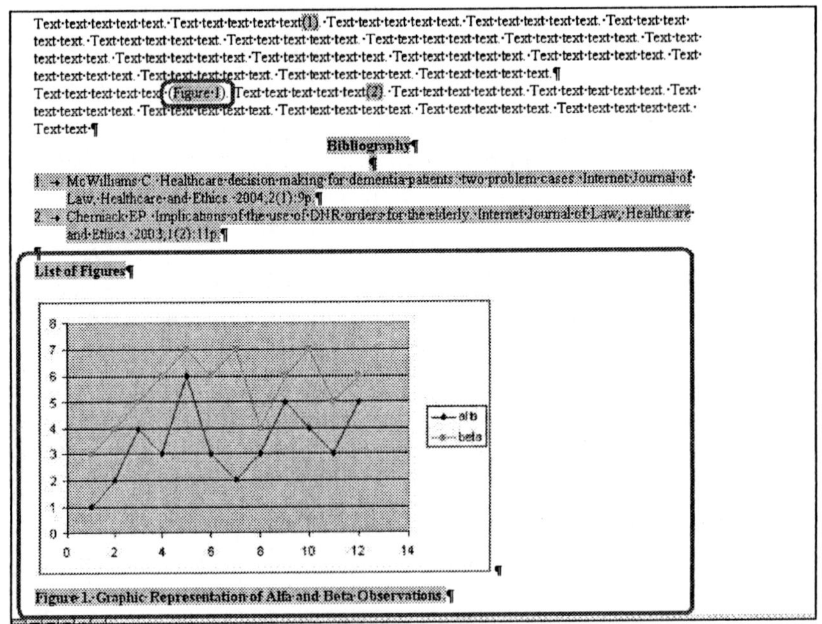

EndNote creates an in-text citation, a heading for the list of graphs, the graph itself and a caption label near the graph. The insertion of graphs is instantly formatted in conformity with the current Style. In the example above the Style is set to create the list of figures at the end of the document and the caption label below the graph.

Tables and Figures are listed separately and are displayed after the bibliography. In some instances the bibliography is placed after the List of Tables but before the List of Figures. If so, the bibliography can easily be moved with cut and paste and the bibliography will keep its position as long as unformatting of citations has not taken place.

After having inserted some citations, figures, and tables and then formatted the bibliography the document may look like this:

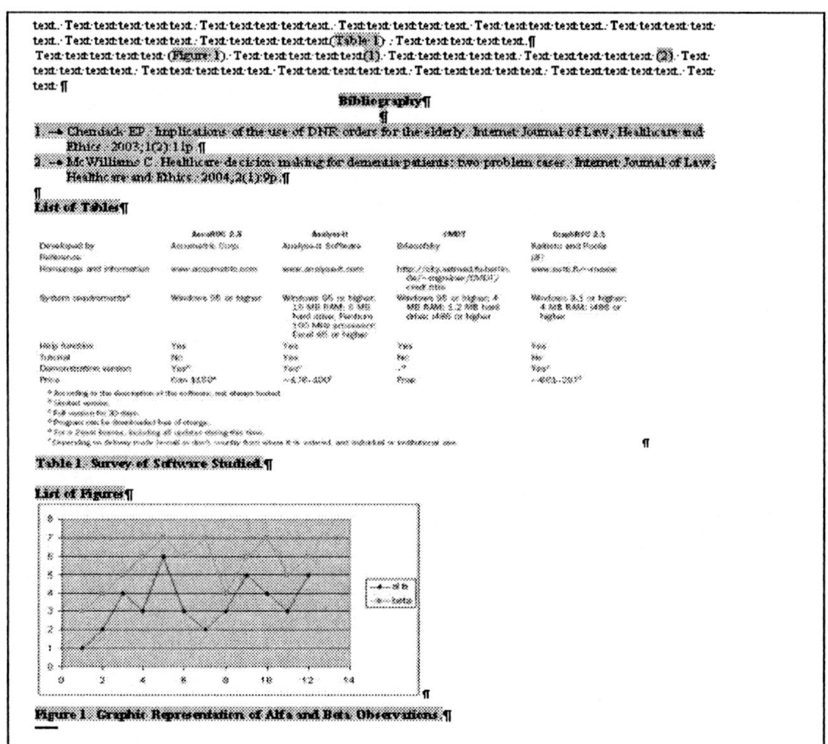

text.·Text·text·text·text·text.·Text·text·text·text·text.·Text·text·text·text·text.·Text·text·text·text·text.·Text·text·text·text·text.·Text·text·text·text·text.·Text·text·text·text·text(Table·1)·.Text·text·text·text·text.¶
Text·text·text·text·text·(Figure·1).·Text·text·text·text·text(1).·Text·text·text·text·text.·Text·text·text·text·text·(2).·Text·text·text·text·text.·Text·text·text·text·text.·Text·text·text·text·text.·Text·text·text·text·text.·Text·text·text·text·text.·Text·text·¶

Bibliography¶

¶

1. → Chendack·EP.·Implications·of·the·use·of·DNR·orders·for·the·elderly.·Internet·Journal·of·Law,·Healthcare·and·Ethics.·2003;1(2):11p.¶
2. → McWilliams·C.·Healthcare·decision·making·for·dementia·patients:·two·problem·cases.·Internet·Journal·of·Law,·Healthcare·and·Ethics.·2004;2(1):9p.¶

¶

List·of·Tables¶

¶

Table·1.·Survey·of·Software·Studied.¶

List·of·Figures¶

¶

Figure·1.·Graphic·Representation·of·Alfa·and·Beta·Observations.¶

The editing options in a Word manuscript for figures and tables are: moving the position of the in-text label, deleting the in-text label (and the whole graph), and adding new graphs. Even though instant formatting always applies for figures and tables there is a need to refresh the lists of figures and tables after moving and deleting graphs. If the Style has been changed or modified a refresh will also be necessary.

Refresh is made by **Tools - EndNote α**[14] **- Generate Figure List** or with the icon [icon].

Resizing and rotating[15] the graphs with normal Word commands is often necessary. Such resizing is restored after refresh of the figure and table lists.

[14] Where α represents 7, 8, 9, or X depending on the EndNote-version.

[15] Inserting charts and figures with EndNote gives the same result as the Word command Insert Picture From File (without link): a Picture object (Windows Metafile) which can be resized and rotated (in other layout modes than *In line with text*).

If a record with a graphics file needs to be edited, like for example when the text in the caption field must be changed then the above refresh will not have an effect. In such cases the previous in-text label must be deleted and replaced and the modified record inserted.

The settings of the current Style determine the layout of tables and figures. The current Style can easily be opened with the shortcut command **Edit - Output Styles - Edit "current Style"**.

Choose **Figures** alt. **Tables** under **Figures & Tables** and the following options display:

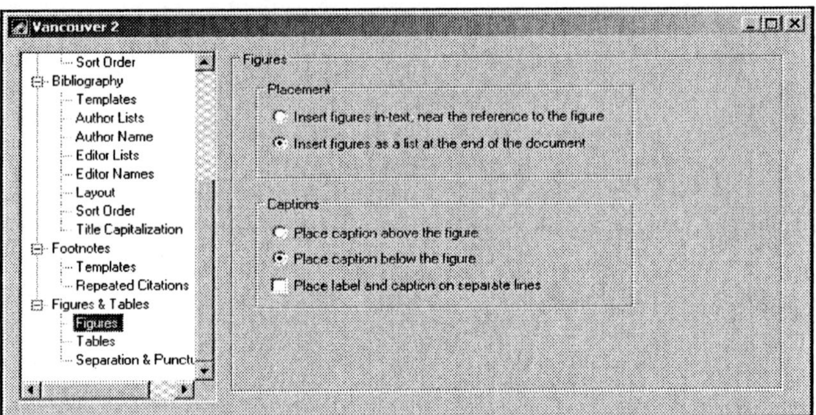

The option *Insert figures/tables in-text...* means that such graphs will be placed immediately after the paragraph where the in-text label has been placed. The text **List of Figures/Tables** will not display. Choose **Separation & Punctuation** under **Figures & Charts** and the following options will display:

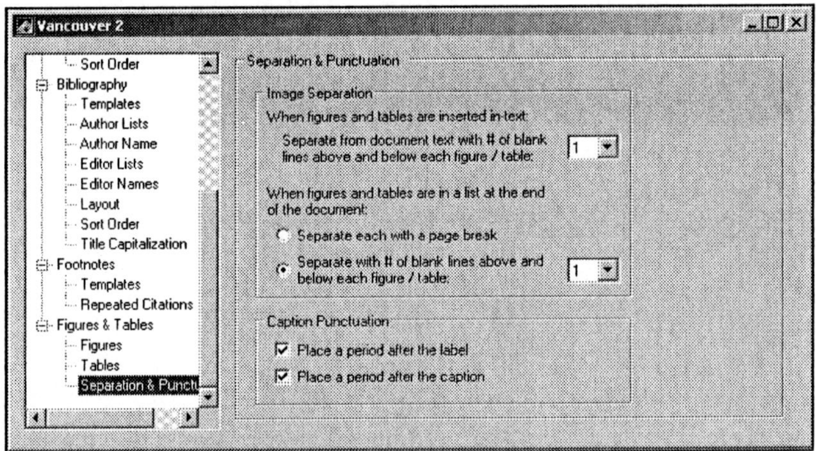

Each modification of a Style must be saved by EndNote with **File - Save** followed by **Return to Word** and refresh with **Tools - EndNote α[16] - Generate Figure List** or with the icon .

[16] Where α represents 7, 8, 9, or X depending on the EndNote-version.

8. INSERTING NOTES

At times there is a need of inserting notes which are not bibliographic references but are listed and numbered as in text citations and are sorted among the items of the bibliography.

- **Follow These Steps**

    1 From Word go to **Tools - EndNote α[17] - Insert Note...** or key command **[Alt] + [0]**
    or the icon .
    The following box appears:

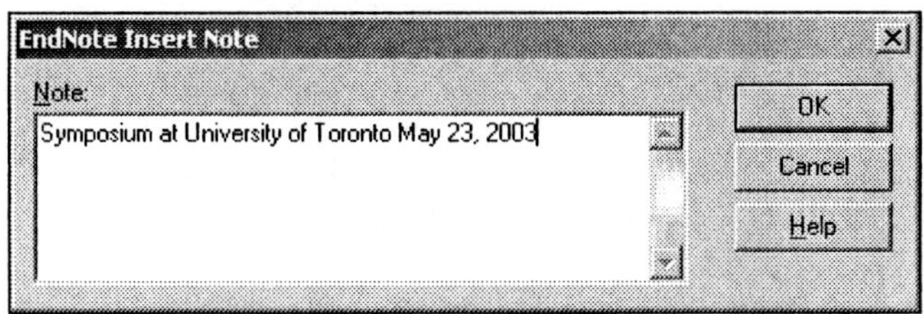

    2 Type the note and apply **[OK]**.

The syntax of unformatted citation is:

`{NOTE:Symposium at University of Toronto May 23, 2003}`

Depending on the Style the result after having formatted the bibliography may be as follows:

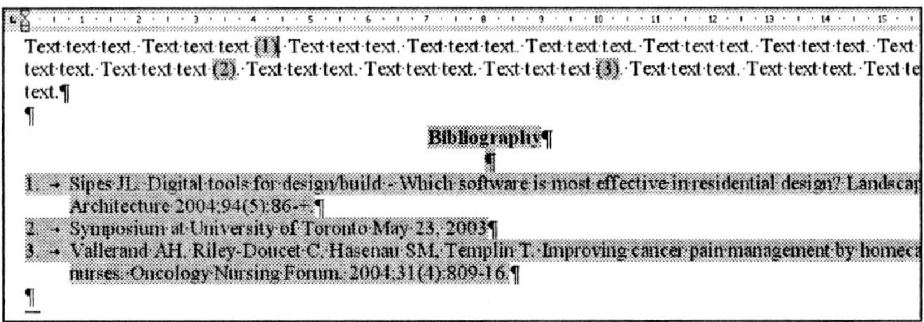

Text text text. Text text text (1). Text text text. Text text text. Text text text. Text text text. Text text text. Text text text. Text text text (2). Text text text. Text text text. Text text text (3). Text text text. Text text text. Text te text.

Bibliography

1. Sipes JL. Digital tools for design/build - Which software is most effective in residential design? Landscap Architecture 2004;94(5):86-+.
2. Symposium at University of Toronto May 23, 2003
3. Vallerand AH, Riley-Doucet C, Hasenau SM, Templin T. Improving cancer pain management by homec nurses. Oncology Nursing Forum. 2004;31(4):809-16.

For formatting the bibliography, see Chapter 9, page 51.

[17] Where α represents 7, 8, 9, or X depending on the EndNote-version.

9. CREATING BIBLIOGRAPHIES

Formatting Bibliographies

Format Bibliography is the command that creates a bibliography as an integral part of a manuscript.

- ♦ **Follow These Steps**

1 You need to open the Word document and the EndNote Library or Libraries from where you have inserted the citation(s).

From Word:

2 Go to **Tools** - **EndNote α**[18] - **Format Bibliography...**
or key command **[Alt]** + **[3]**
or the icon .

From EndNote:

2 Go to **Tools** - **Cite While You Write [CWYW]** - **Format Bibliography...**
or key command **[Alt]** + **[3]**
or the icon .

This dialog box lets you control the appearance of the bibliography.

Format Bibliography tab:

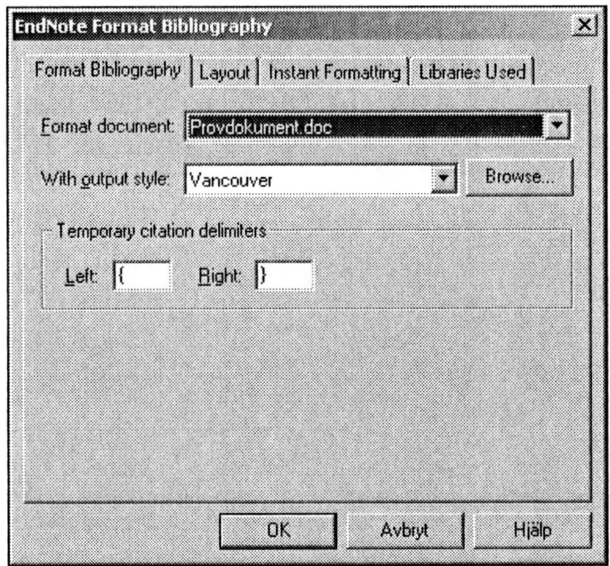

- **Format document:** The file name of the current document is displayed. All other open documents are listed in the drop-down list.
- **With output style:** The current style is in active position and other Style Favorites are listed. More styles are available from the **[Browse...]**-button.
- **Temporary citation delimiters:** will display the default settings from **Edit** - **Preferences** – **Temporary Citations**, see page 17.

[18] Where α represents 7, 8, 9, or X depending on the EndNote-version.

Layout tab:

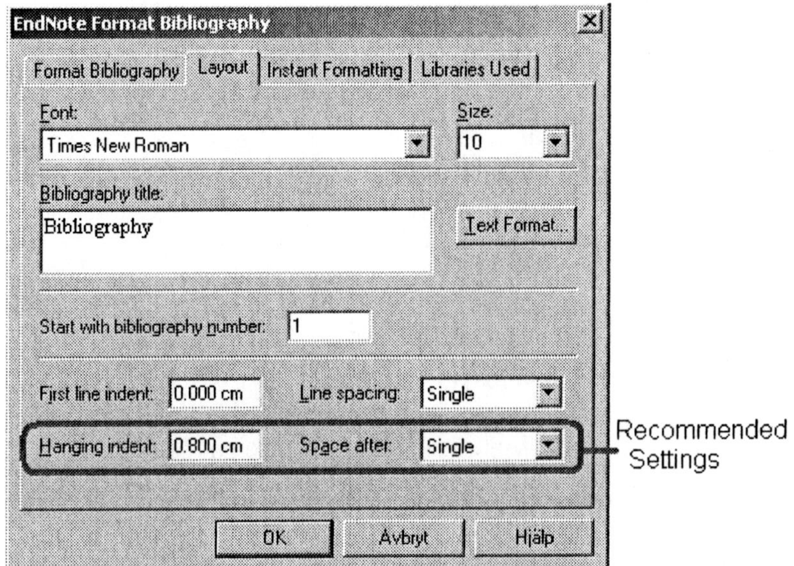

- **Bibliography Title:** You may type for example `Bibliography` which will be displayed in the document as a result of the formatting. Text attributes apply with the **[Text Format...]**-button. The title is always center aligned.
- **First line indent:** Default value is 0.000 but any positive value between 0.000 and 8.000 in may be chosen.
- **Hanging Indent:** May easily be modified to any suitable value, e.g. 0.8 cm
- **Space after:** It is often recommended to select *Single* in order to create more space between references.

Instant Formatting tab:

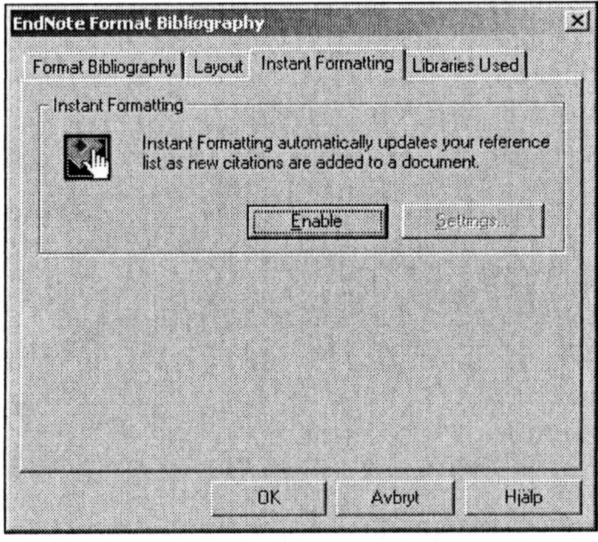

The default setting is inherited from the settings made in Cite While You Write Preferences, see page 18.

Libraries Used tab:

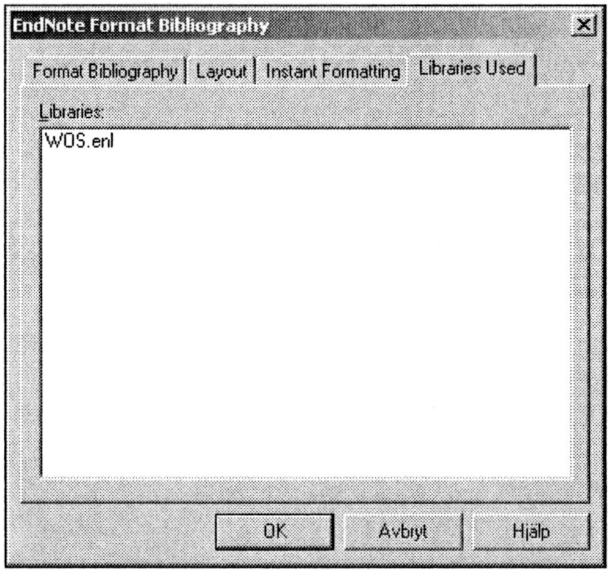

The libraries used for one specific document are listed. Even if formatting without an open library is possible due to the Traveling Library feature described on page 71, it is recommended that the library or libraries referred to should be open during formatting.

- ♦ -

All the above settings are specific and stored individually for each document. When a new document is opened the settings are the system default values. Most of the default settings are made in EndNote **CWYW Preferences** on page 18 and some other settings are made in **Edit - Preferences** from the main menu.

Finally, for any formatting to take effect, confirm with the **[OK]**-button.

The result, depending on the current style, may be like this:

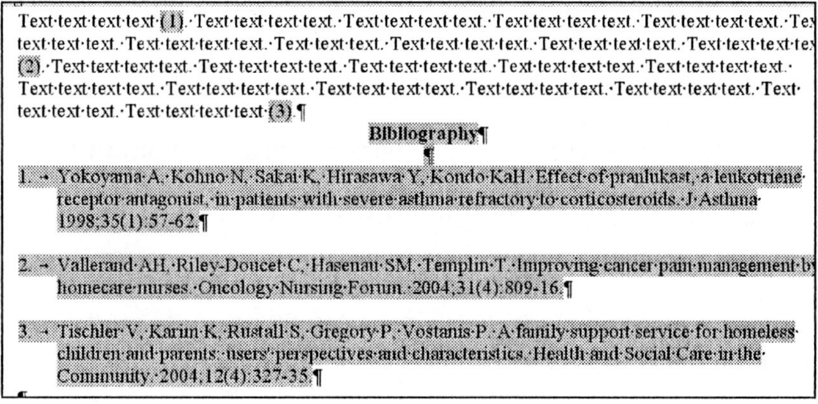

Text text text text (1). Text text text text. Text text text text. Text text text text. Text text text text. Te text text text. Text text text text. Text text text. Text text text text. Text text text text. Text text text te (2). Text text text text. Text text text text. Text text text text. Text text text text. Text text text text. Text text text text. Text text text text. Text text text text. Text text text text. Text text text text. Text text text text. Text text text text (3).

Bibliography

1. Yokoyama A, Kohno N, Sakai K, Hirasawa Y, Kondo KaH. Effect of pranlukast, a leukotriene receptor antagonist, in patients with severe asthma refractory to corticosteroids. J Asthma 1998;35(1):57-62.
2. Vallerand AH, Riley-Doucet C, Hasenau SM, Templin T. Improving cancer pain management by homecare nurses. Oncology Nursing Forum. 2004;31(4):809-16.
3. Tischler V, Karim K, Rustall S, Gregory P, Vostanis P. A family support service for homeless children and parents: users' perspectives and characteristics. Health and Social Care in the Community. 2004;12(4):327-35.

The position of the bibliography is always after the last paragraph of the document when a bibliography is first formatted. If a different position is required, possibly before attachments like figures and tables, the whole bibliography may be moved with cut and paste into its new position. When Format Bibliography (refresh) is applied the bibliography will stay in its position. As soon as the Unformat Citation(s) command is applied, however, the bibliography will restore to its default position after the last paragraph upon subsequent formatting.

When Things Go Wrong

On occasions after selecting the Format Bibliography command the following **EndNote Select Matching Refence** dialog box might appear:

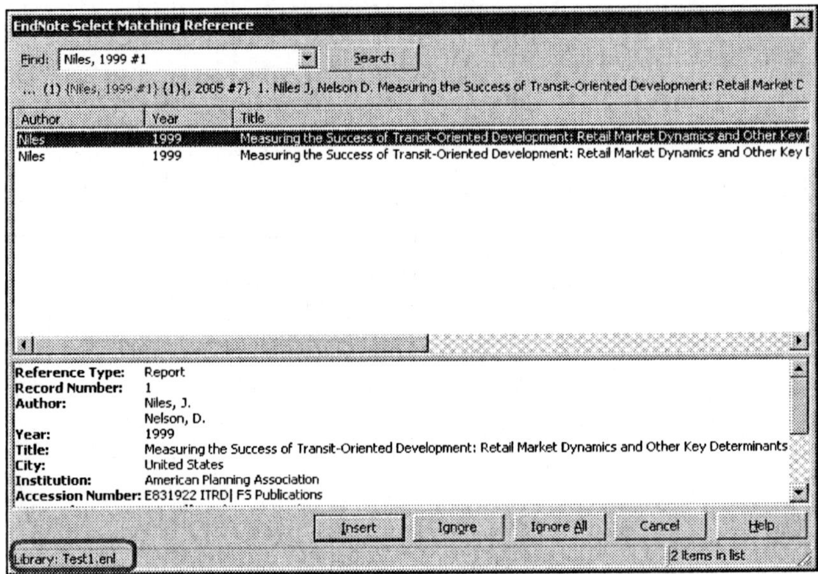

The reason why this dialogue box appears is because EndNote is unable to determine which reference should be used for a particular citation. The first time the Format Bibliography command is applied EndNote refers to the information from the temporary citation (type **`{Cherniack, 2003 #243}`**, see page 40) and searches for that reference in the currently open library.

EndNote may be unable to identify a certain reference for one of the following reasons:

- The library with the inserted citation is not open.
- The reference is missing from the current open library (the inserted reference may have been a duplicate which subsequently may have been deleted from the library).
- The reference in the library may have been modified after it was inserted.
- The reference exists in several open libraries with same record number.

The items shown in the dialog box are suggestions by EndNote and the user can decide by highlighting the correct item, and insert again with the **[Insert]**-button. The library of the highlighted item is shown in the lower left corner of the dialog box.

[Ignore] means no action and the formatting carries on to the next citation.

[Cancel] discontinues the formatting.

Creating a Bibliography from Several Documents

In case you want to merge several documents into one after having written any number of chapters of a book or separate sections of an article you also want to create a common bibliography with citations from the various chapters or sections.

There are a few methods to choose from. Common for all methods is that all separate documents which are going to be merged must have *unformatted citations* before being merged.

For your main Word document, use any of the following methods:

- Use Word's Master Document feature.
- Insert file (note, *without link* to inserted document).
- Copy and paste from one document to another.

After merging all documents the usual Format Bibliography command will apply. Later you can add the contents from one more document which also needs to be *unformatted* before inserted or pasted into the main document.

Independent Bibliographies

An independent bibliography is a list of references that is not generated from citations in a paper but more self-generated. There are several occasions (literature list, order list, CV) when an independent bibliography is needed. EndNote offers various procedures, output styles and file formats.

The common principle for all procedures is that the current output style determines the format including text attributes, indenting, numbering, sorting etceteras.

Copy Formatted

EndNote has a unique feature called Copy Formatted. This command means that highlighted references are copied to the clipboard and formatted according to the current output style. In case several references are copied the sorting determined by the output style that prevails. If the sort order is Order of Appearance then sorting will be according to the order in which the references were highlighted.

♦ **Follow These Steps**

1. Activate the current library.
2. Select an Output Style.
3. Highlight selected reference(s).
4. Go to **Edit - Copy Formatted**
   or key command **[Ctrl]** + **[K]**
   or right-click the mouse and select **Copy Formatted**.

The independent bibliography is now in the Windows clipboard and can be pasted into Word or any word processor, an e-mail, or virtually any other Windows application.

The Copy Formatted command cannot store paragraph attributes like indenting or line spacing. Text attributes, however, like bold, italic, underline and tabs are determined by the current output style.

Printing References

- **Follow These Steps**
  1. Activate the current library.
  2. Select an Output Style.
  3. Highlight selected reference(s)
  4. Go to **File - Print**
     or key command **[Ctrl]** + **[P]**
     or the icon .
  5. Confirm current printer settings.

When there is a need to print *only one reference* in accordance with the display of the Reference windows including all displayed field names a special routine prevails which is *independent* from the current output style.

- **Follow These Steps**
  1. Activate the current library.
  2. Open the selected reference.
  3. Go to **File - Print**
     or key command **[Ctrl]** + **[P]**
     or the icon .
  4. Confirm current printer settings.

Subject Bibliographies and Subject Lists

A subject bibliography is an independent bibliography consisting of sections of literature references under separate headings and sorted according to certain criteria. The headings used are selected terms from the collection of references and can be any type of term such as authors, keywords, journals etc.

A subject list is simply the list of selected headings but without the bibliographies. A subject list can be with or without subject term count which makes it possible to make simple frequency studies of selected references.

Practical uses of subject bibliographies are lists of journal abstracts, current awareness lists, subject indexes, or lists of holdings by category. When author names are used as subject headings this feature easily produces lists of literature for use in any CV.

The selection of records in a certain library that shall be used when creating a Subject Bibliography or Subject List is determined as follows.

EndNote 7 and earlier versions: If no records are highlighted then all records will be included otherwise it will only be the highlighted ones.

EndNote 8 and later versions: The currently shown records are used. That could mean the result of any search in a library or the result of highlighting selected records followed by **References - Show Selected References**.

Here are two examples of a practical use of Subject Bibliographies.

Example 1 – Subject Bibliography - Authors' Bibliography

- **Follow These Steps**
  1. Open the current library.
  2. Select the records to be included in the subject bibliography. See page 56 how to select records.
  3. Go to **Tools - Subject Bibliography...**
  4. Highlight *Author.*

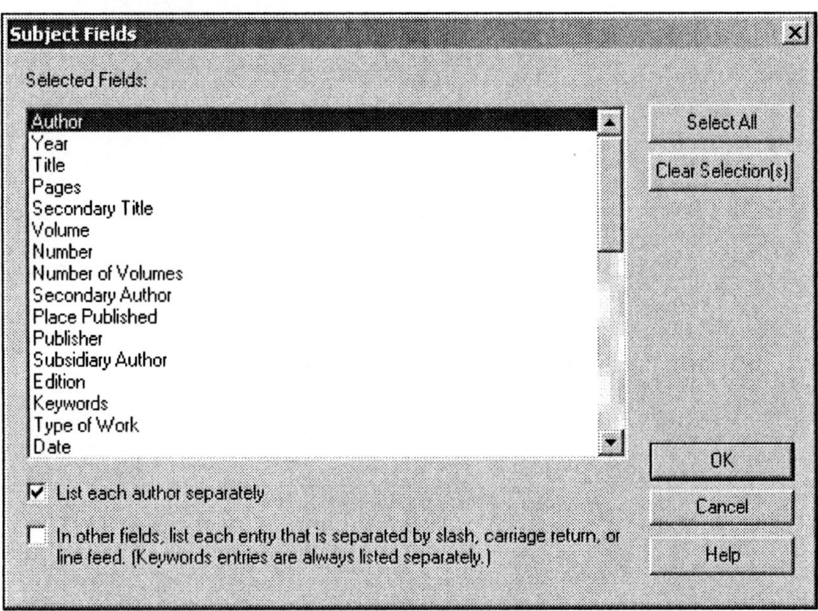

  5. Confirm with **[OK]**.
  6. In the Subject Terms highlight the requested author name(s). The default sort order is alphabetical. Sorting according to number of records (occurrence rate) is made by clicking on the [**#Records**]-button. Repeated click reverses the sort order.

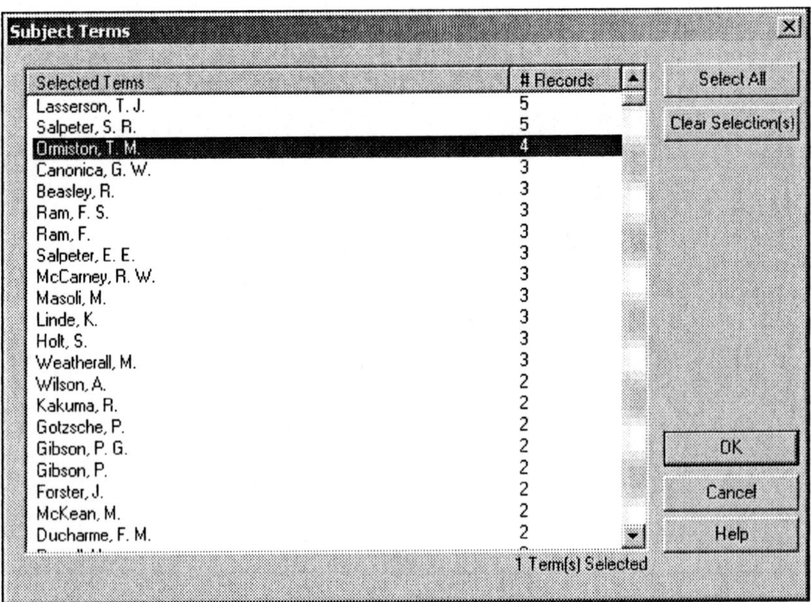

7 Confirm with **[OK]**.

The result, depending on settings, may be like this:

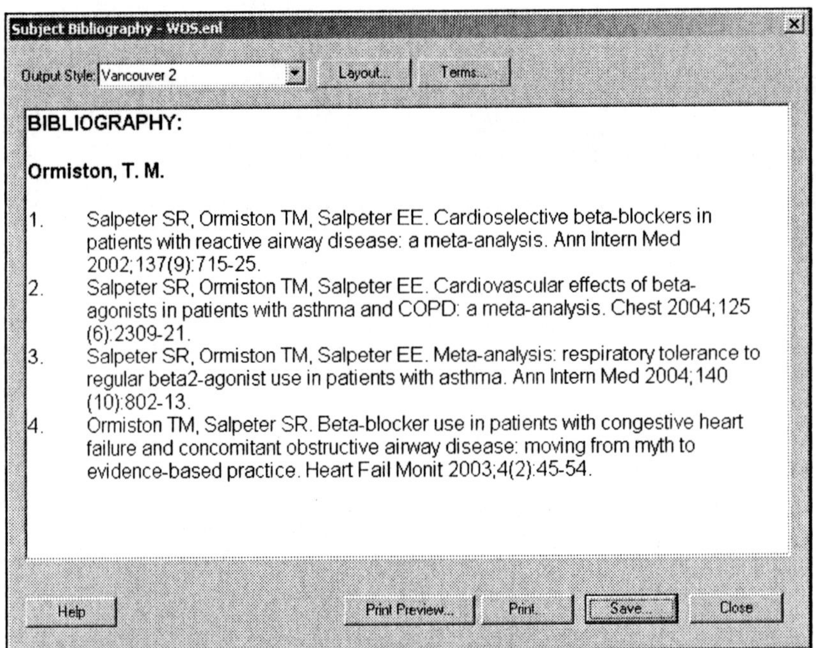

The **[Layout]**-button leads us to the Configure Subject Bibliography settings window with four alternative tabs:

References tab:

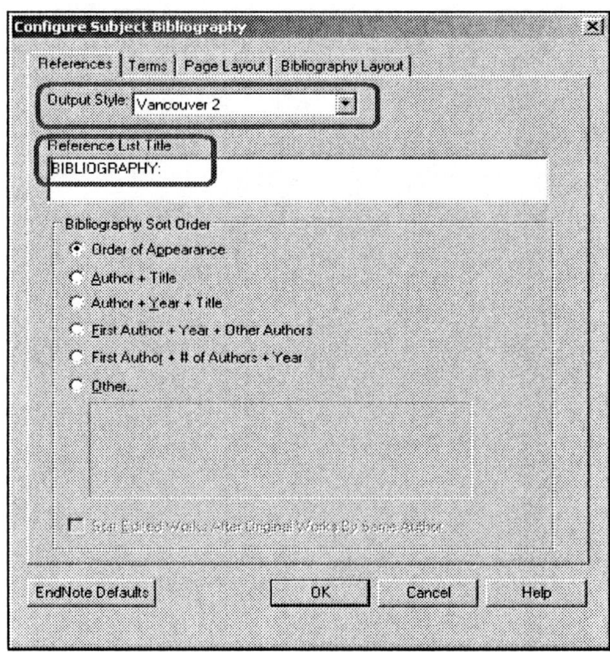

The default Output Style can be changed by selecting another style from the drop-down list. The title **BIBLIOGRAPHY** has been typed in the Reference List Title box.

Terms tab:

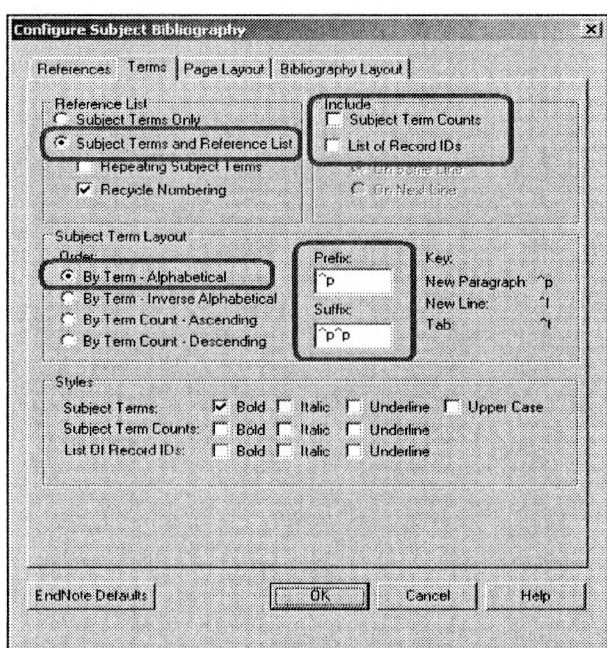

Subject Terms and Reference List has been selected.

Page Layout tab:

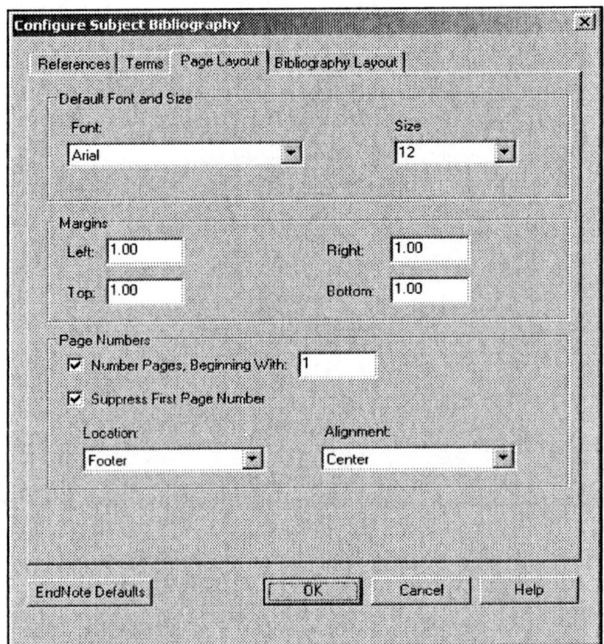

The default settings have been accepted.
Bibliography Layout tab:

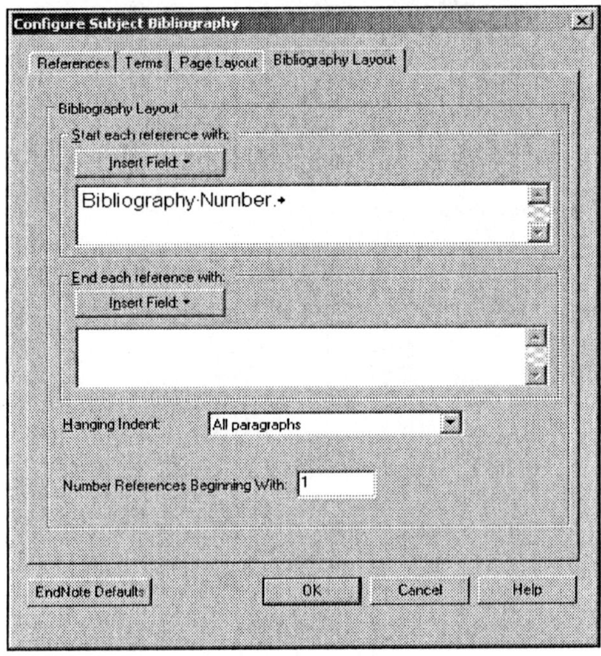

The default settings have been accepted.

Finally, when all settings for all tabs are accepted, confirm with **[OK]**. The settings are stored in EndNote until new changes are made. Restore EndNote default settings for individual tabs with the **[EndNote Defaults]**-button.

Example 2 – Subject List - Frequency Study of Substances

♦ **Follow These Steps**

1. Open the current library.
2. Select the records to be included in the subject bibliography. See page 56 how to select records.
3. Go to **Tools – Subject Bibliography...**
4. Highlight *Custom 2*, which in this example corresponds to the field Substances.
5. Check *In other fields*... since this particular field is neither Author nor Keywords.

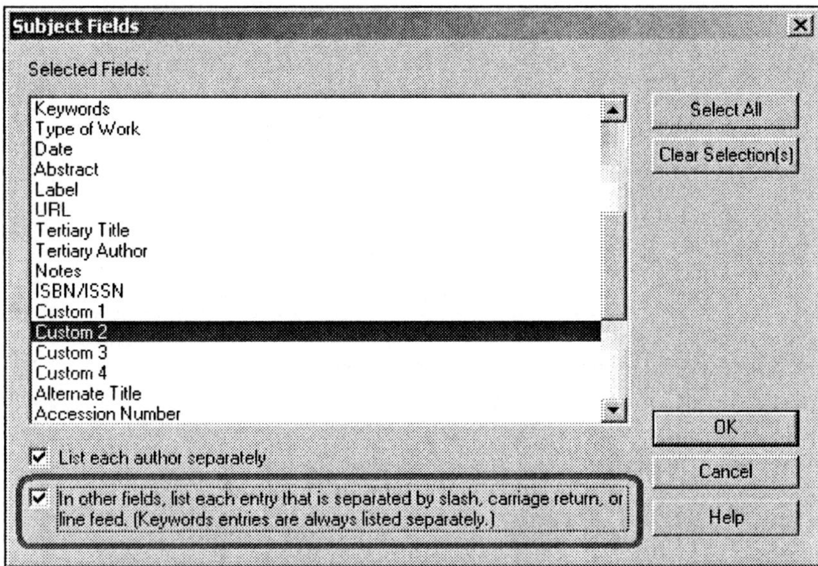

6. In the Subject Terms window highlight the terms of interest for the current study.

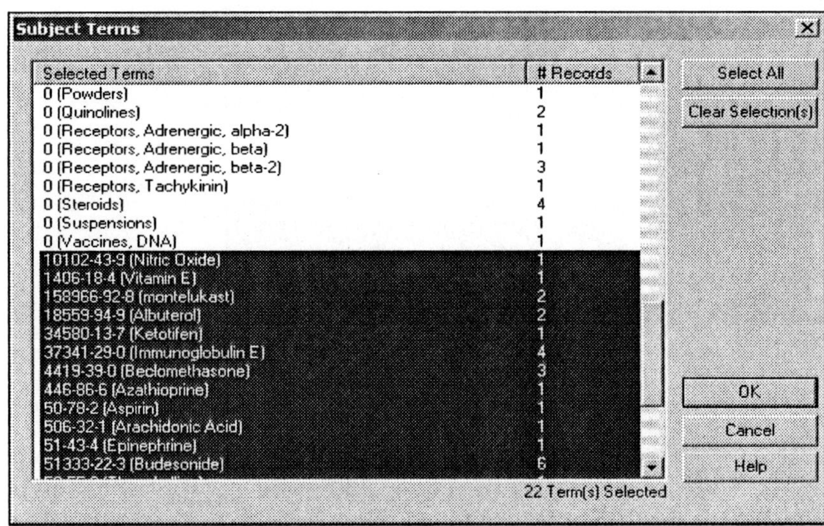

7. Confirm with **[OK]**.

The result, depending on settings, may be like this:

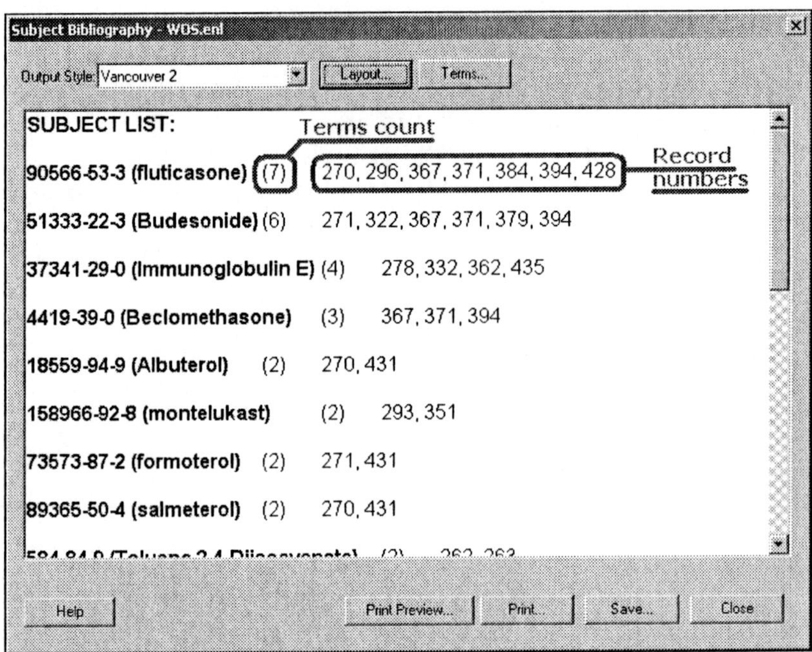

The [**Layout**]-button leads us to the Configure Subject Bibliography window and we comment on some settings specific for this example.

References tab:

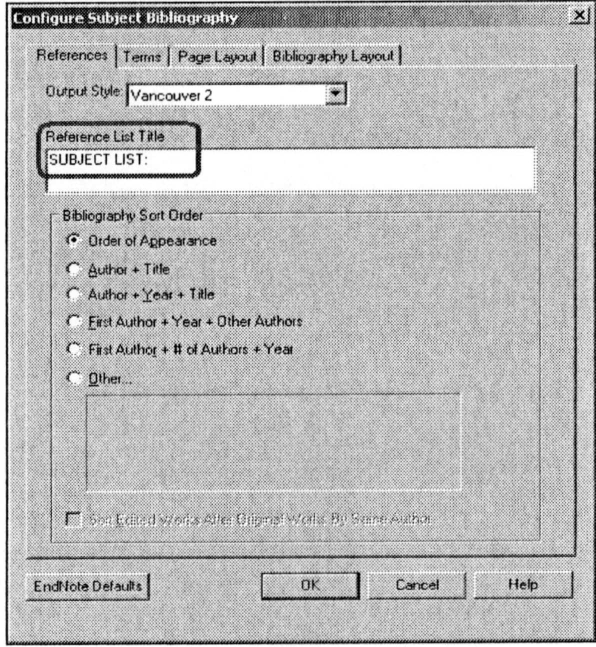

We have modified the title to read **SUBJECT LIST**.

Terms tab:

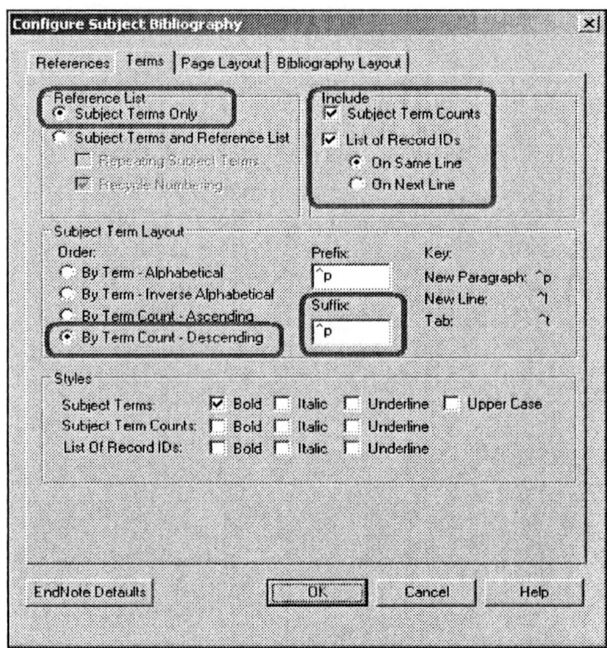

We selected *Subject Terms Only, Subject Term Counts, and List of Record IDs.* Sort order is by *Term Count, Descending.*

The default settings for the **Page Layout** and **Bibliography Layout** tabs have been accepted.

Finally, when all the settings for all tabs are selected, confirm with [**OK**]. The settings are stored in EndNote until new changes are made. Restore EndNote default settings for each individual tab with the [**EndNote Defaults**]-button.

- ♦ -

Finally, when the Subject Bibliography window displays an acceptable result, use the [**Print Preview...**], [**Print...**], or [**Save...**]-buttons for alternative outputs.

10. EDITING CITATIONS

Deleting, moving, or adding inserted citations should always be made in the text block of the Word document, no matter if the citation is formatted or temporary. A refresh is made with the Format Bibliography command.

Deleting Citations

A citation is deleted exactly as normal text is deleted. Editing a composite citation is a bit more complicated. A composite citation of the type `[1-3]` may require that one of the three references shall be deleted. Two methods are at hand:

Method 1

- **Follow These Steps**
  1 Place the cursor in the composite, formatted citation you intend to modify.
  2 Go to **Tools - EndNote α**[19] **- Edit Citation(s)**
  or **[Alt]** + **[6]**
  or the icon [icon].

You will now see all the citations of your document displayed and the first reference in the composite citation is highlighted:

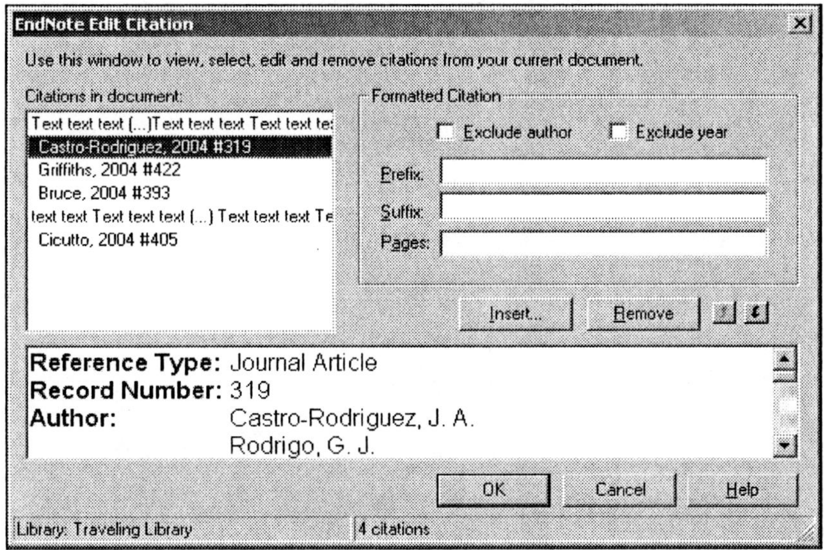

  3 Highlight the reference(s) you want to delete.
  4 Delete with **[Remove]**.
  5 Confirm with **[OK]**.

The immediate result of this operation is the temporary citation:
`{Castro-Rodriguez, 2004 #319;Bruce, 2004 #393}`
and after formatting (refresh) the final result will become: `[1, 2]`

You may highlight any reference and use the **[Remove]**-button to remove or the **[Insert...]**-button to add a new reference. With the

[19] Where α represents 7, 8, 9, or X depending on the EndNote-version.

Arrow-buttons you may move one reference up or down within same composite citation.

Method 2

- **Follow These Steps**
  1. Highlight the citation you need to modify.
  2. Go to **Tools - EndNote α**[20] **- Unformat Citation(s)** or **[Alt]** + **[4]** or the icon
  3. Edit directly in the temporary citation the reference you want to delete. Be careful and maintain the syntax.

After formatting (refresh) the desired result is achieved.

Prefix and Suffix in a Citation

Sometimes there is a need to add a prefix or a suffix to an individual citation.

Example: The formatted citation is `[4]`. The author wants to add a prefix and a suffix so that the citation will become
`[See especially 4, pages 24-25]`.

- **Follow These Steps**
  1. Place the cursor in the composite, formatted citation you need to modify.
  2. Go to **Tools - EndNote α - Edit Citation(s)** or **[Alt]** + **[6]** or the icon
  3. Type the required Prefix and Suffix in the respective text boxes. Consider spaces if needed.

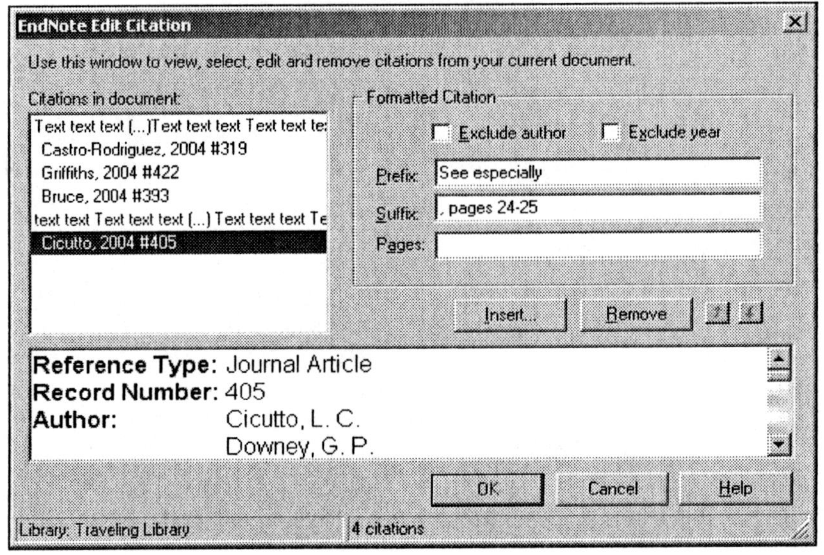

  4. Confirm with **[OK]**.

The immediate result of this operation is the temporary citation:
`{See especially \Cicutto, 2004 #405, pages 24-25}`

[20] Where α represents 7, 8, 9, or X depending on the EndNote-version.

and after formatting (refresh) the result becomes:
`[See especially 4, pages 24-25]`

The textbox under **Pages:** is used when Cited Pages are defined in a Style, see page 82.

Adding and Merging Citations

Adding one reference to an existing citation which should form a composite or a merged citation is very easy.

♦ **Follow These Steps**

1. Position the cursor immediately before or after the existing citation and apply no space in between.
2. Insert the new citation.

The immediate result is:
`[3]{Cicutto, 2004 #405}`
and after formatting (refresh) the final result will become: `[3,4]`.

11. UNFORMATTING CITATION(S)

Unformat Citation(s) means that the whole document or one particular citation is restored back to a temporary citation. The Unformat Citation(s) command is only available from Word.

When you need to unformat the whole document:

- **Follow These Steps**
  1. Place the cursor anywhere in a formatted document and let no highlighting include a formatted citation.
  2. Go to **Tools - EndNote α**[21] **- Unformat Citation(s)** or key command **[Alt]** + [4] or the icon .

When you need to unformat only one specific citation:

- **Follow These Steps**
  1. Highlight the citation you need to unformat.
  2. Go to **Tools - EndNote α - Unformat Citation(s)** or key command **[Alt]** + [4] or the icon .

[21] Where α represents 7, 8, 9, or X depending on the EndNote-version.

12. TRAVELING LIBRARY

A Traveling Library is a function that stores bibliographic data from the inserted references in a Word document in the form of embedded field codes. The Abstract, Notes and Image fields are not included in a traveling library.

The first time a citation is formatted the corresponding Library must be open. Later when any reformatting takes place the bibliographic data is captured from the traveling library. After unformatting citation(s) the EndNote Library needs to be open before formatting can take place again.

This means that it is possible to send a formatted document to a computer that has EndNote α[22] installed but not the same Library. This computer may even re-format and use another Style. But as soon as the document is unformatted and saved then an open Library with these references must be open in order to format again.

The embedded field codes may be exported from a Word document to an EndNote library with all bibliographic data. Such a traveling library will not have the same record numbers as the originally used library which is why it cannot be fully used with the document until all earlier citations have been replaced with records from the traveling library.

From Word:

Go to **Tools - EndNote α - Export Traveling Library...**

or key command **[Alt] + [8]**

or the icon :

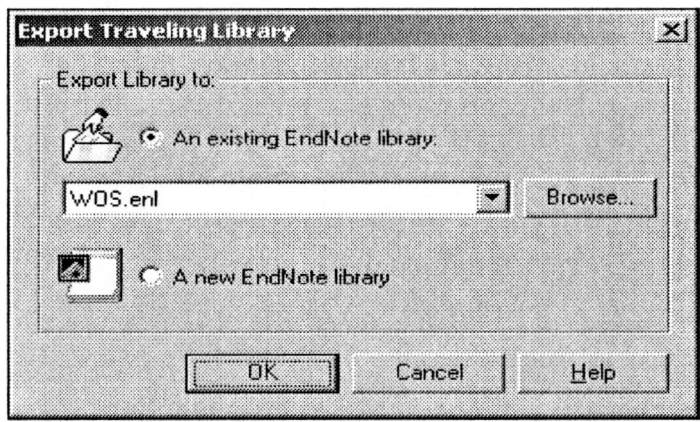

[22] Where α represents 7, 8, 9, or X depending on the EndNote-version.

From EndNote:
Go to **Tools - Cite While You Write [CWYW] - Import Traveling Library...**
or key command **[Alt] + [8]**:

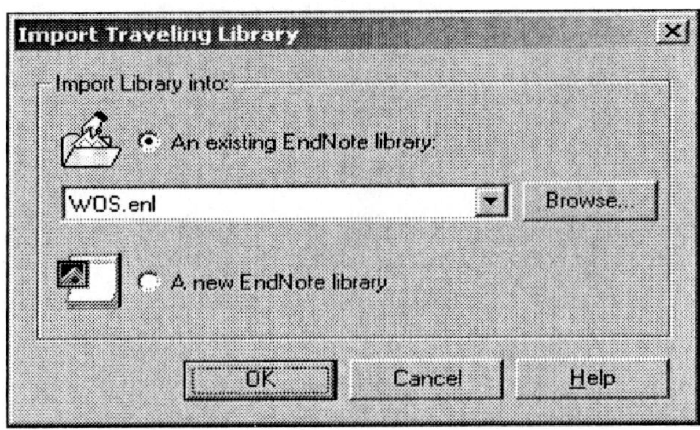

Finally, select a new or an existing library for the import.

Sending a Word-document between Users

At times there is a need to send documents between users for proofreading, adding comments, or as information. The best format to use depends on how the parties work together and if same version of EndNote and respectively Word are used. The best guarantee for a reliable exchange of information is when all parties use the same version of both software. It is recommended but not imperative that both the Word-document and the EndNote library travel together and are updated by one particular user at a time.

If the receiver uses EndNote α[23] but not the same EndNote-library as the sender it is quite safe to send the formatted Word-document and benefit from the simplicity of the Traveling Library.

Should a proofreader, who does not use EndNote, edit the text it is far safer to send a Word-document without field codes as described for the Publisher's Copy on page 89. Changes made should be inserted in the master document with great care. We suggest using the Word features under **Tools - Track Changes** and/or **Compare Documents** or under **Insert - Comment**.

Compatibility between Documents

Users of different versions of EndNote must observe the following aspects of a Traveling Library. A formatted document that uses EndNote 8 or later cannot be subject to the reformatting or the exporting of the Traveling Library when the new user has EndNote 7 or earlier. A document created by EndNote 7 or earlier can however be reformatted by a user of EndNote 8 or later who may also export the Traveling Library. Various versions of Word are however not critical in respect of the Traveling Library.

[23] Where α represents 7, 8, 9, or X depending on the EndNote-version.

13. EDITING LIBRARY REFERENCE(S)

Sometimes you will need to open a certain library reference from the position of an in-text citation. This will also make it possible to edit the reference(s).

- **Follow These Steps**
  1. Place the cursor in the citation(s), formatted or temporary.
  2. Go to **Tools - EndNote α**[24] **- Edit Library Reference(s)** or key command **[Alt]** + **[5]** or the icon .
  3. You can now edit the reference, and close it.
  4. Return to Word with **Tools - Cite While You Write [CWYW] - Return to Word** or key command **[Alt]** + **[1]** or the icon .
     The citation is now unformatted.
  5. Re-format (refresh) with **Tools - EndNote α - Format Bibliography** or key command **[Alt]** + **[3]**.

[24] Where α represents 7, 8, 9, or X depending on the EndNote-version.

14. EDITING STYLES

The Output Styles in EndNote are proprietary files holding many different settings that together create the different output formats. These files have the file extension *.ENS for EndNote Style. EndNote is delivered with a large number (more than 1000) of prepared output styles. These styles differ in terms of their function and can be divided into two different groups: The *bibliographic formats* representing author instructions from a certain publisher or journal and the *utility formats* that can be used for printout, easy reading, document ordering, or export of data. EndNote incorporates all necessary tools to edit or create new such output styles.

The instrument to find, select, edit and mark-favorite styles is called the Style Manager and is described below.

Cases may occur when you cannot find one particular Style in EndNote's standard collection. This collection is continuously being expanded with new styles and the latest complete collection is available known as the Style Finder:

http://www.endnote.com/support/enstyles.asp

Searching for a particular style which does not appear in your standard style collection or the Style Finder need not be a big problem. One initial issue is to find the required format described in a clear-cut way. There are several web-sites supporting author instructions, one of them is:

http://kib.ki.se/tools/journals/instructions_authors_en.html

Furthermore, it is worthwhile actually studying the details of the citations and the bibliography of an article from the journal in which you intend to publish your article. Also when you use some of EndNote's standard styles we suggest you verify the output style with an article as minor deviations and imperfections may occur.

Even if the number of variants seem to be overwhelming, a great number of Styles are in fact identical (or nearly identical), even if they carry individual file names.

Using the Preview option of the Style Manager as described on page 84 is useful when you search for a style which is as near your need as possible. Simply open the Style Manager, select the *Preview* option, highlight a certain style and browse with the up or down arrow keys until you find a useful style. If you are lucky then the style could be used as is, otherwise you can modify according to the instructions that follow.

In this section we will give some examples of a few basic principles in editing. Some of the most common minor modifications of Styles are:

- Creating a Hanging Indent
- Changing the in-text citation from parentheses (..) to brackets [..]
- Changing the Title to **Bold**
- Changing the Journal Name to *Italic*
- Deleting the issue number

Compatibility of Styles

Styles created by EndNote 7 or ealier versions can be used by EndNote 8 or later but not vice versa. Any modification saved by EndNote 8 or later preserves a file format of the style which makes it unable to support EndNote 7.

The Style Manager

First we need to choose some favorites among Styles.

♦ **Follow These Steps**

1. Go to **Edit** - **Output Styles** - **Open Style Manager...**
2. Search for your favorites with the [**Find:**]-button, use **By Name...** and type **`vanc`** for Vancouver.
3. Check the small box to the left.

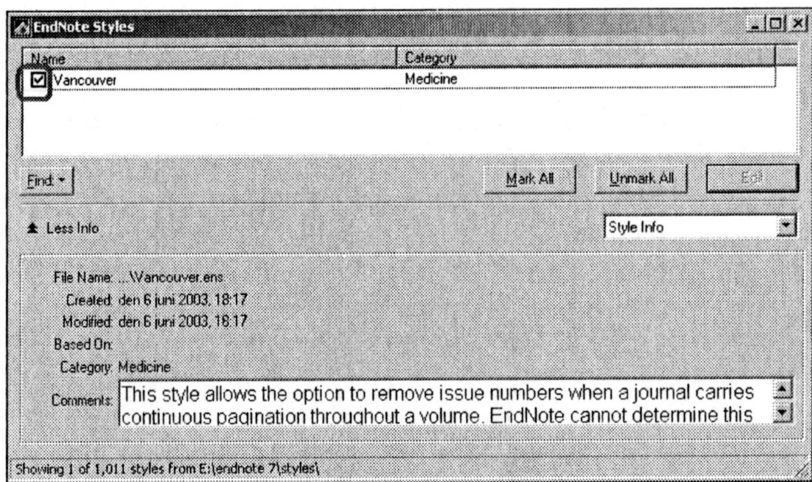

4. Proceed to find next favorite.
5. Close this window with the cross in the upper right-hand corner.

Before you close the Style Manager you can view the list of all selected favorites with the [**Find:**]-button, then **Favorites**. When the Style Manager is closed the favorites are available for easy selection from the drop-down list of the main toolbar:

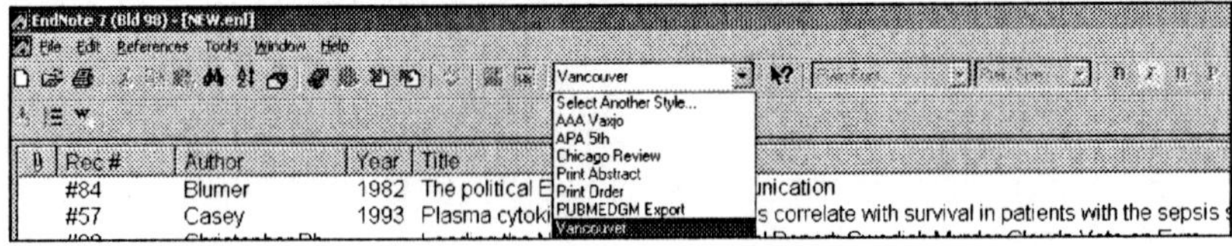

Opening a Style for editing can be made in two ways. The Style Manager is one instrument for doing so. When the Style Manager is open highlight the requested Style and apply The [**Edit**]-button.

We will use the style Vancouver to make the mentioned minor modifications. When Vancouver is the current Style in the drop-down list, there is also a shortcut to edit Vancouver.

- **Follow These Steps**
  1. Go to **Edit - Output Styles - Edit "Vancouver"**.
  2. Make a copy of Vancouver with **File - Save As...**
  3. Name the new copy e.g. Vancouver_mod.
  4. Apply with **[Save]**.

An alternative is creating a new style without any previous settings. Then use **Edit - Output Styles - New Style...** However, in most cases it is much easier to edit an existing style.

In case of a typing error in a new or existing style you may use the undo function **Edit - Undo** or **[Ctrl] + [Z]** to revert to the previously saved instruction for the current field or box. Once a style is saved the undo function will no longer work.

Introducing Hanging indent

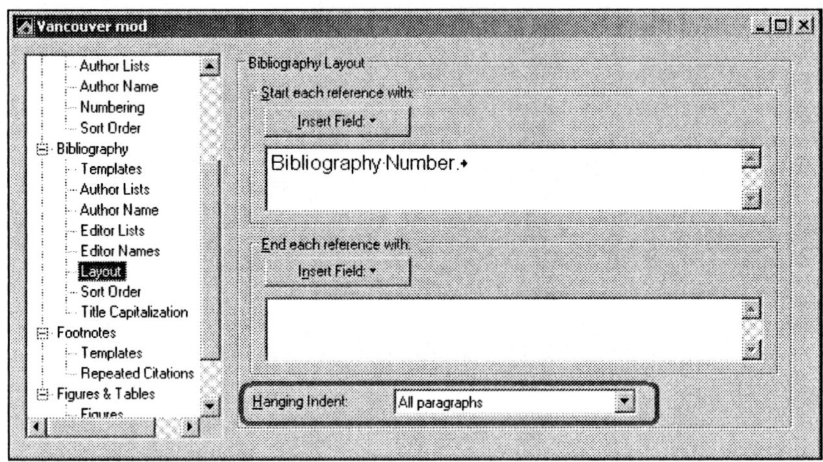

- **Follow These Steps**
  1. Open the Style.
  2. Choose **Bibliography - Layout**.
  3. Select *All paragraphs* from the **Hanging Indent:** drop-down list.
  4. Save settings.

Modifying Citations

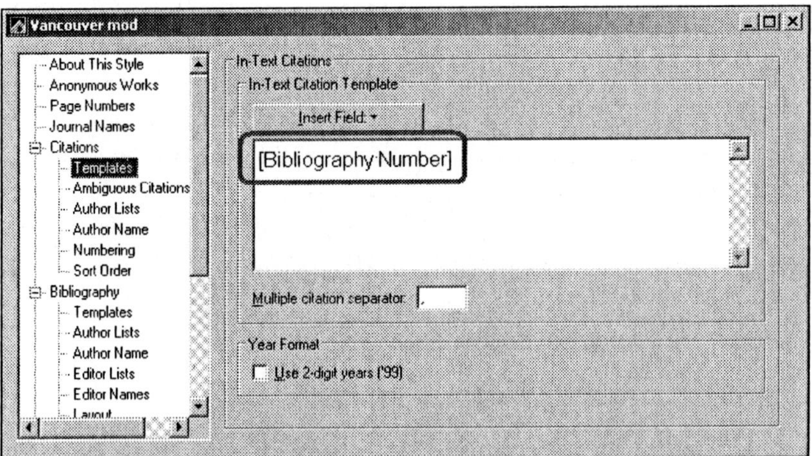

- **Follow These Steps**
  1. Open the Style.
  2. Choose **Citations - Templates.**
  3. Modify directly in the text box by replacing parentheses (..) with brackets [..].
  4. Save settings.

Changing Title to Bold and Journal Name to Italic

The edit mode of **Bibliography - Templates** displays a separate instruction for each existing reference type. The instruction consists of text elements, field elements, and special symbols. When writing or editing such instructions all reference types are available as a list from the button [**Reference Types:**] and as a list with field elements and special symbols from the button [**Insert Field:**]. The special symbols are explained on page 83. Should an instruction for a certain reference type be missing in the list of styles there is a fallback in the form of reference type *Generic* when formatting takes place.

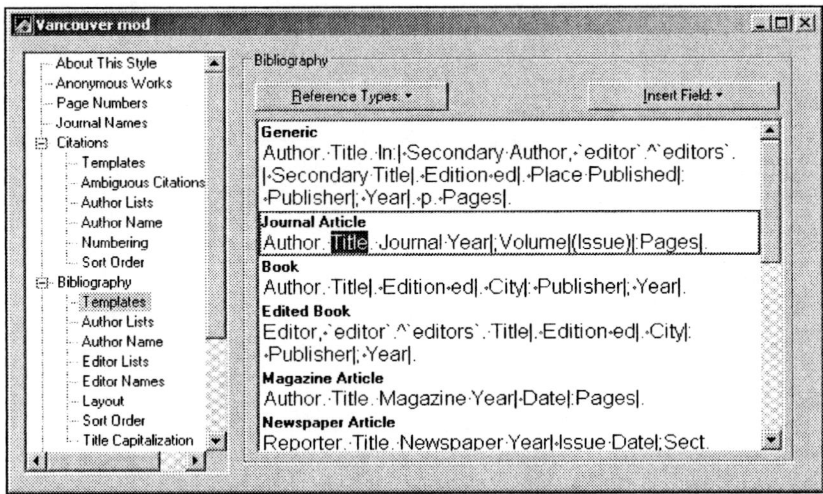

♦ **Follow These Steps**

1. Open the Style.
2. Choose Bibliography - Templates.
3. Highlight *Title* in the Journal Article instruction box.
4. Apply text attribute **Bold.**
5. Highlight *Journal* in the Journal Article instruction box.
6. Apply text attribute *Italic.*
7. Save settings.

Synonyms for Journal Names

In certain instances there are author instructions that require alternative journal names i.e. synonyms to those journal names that are found in the records of an EndNote library. For example the EndNote records may use *N Engl J Med* whereas the instruction requires the format *N. Engl. J. Med.* or *New England Journal of Medicine.*

The solution is to import and use supporting Journal Term Lists as mentioned on page 94. Having imported such term lists the Output style must then be modified.

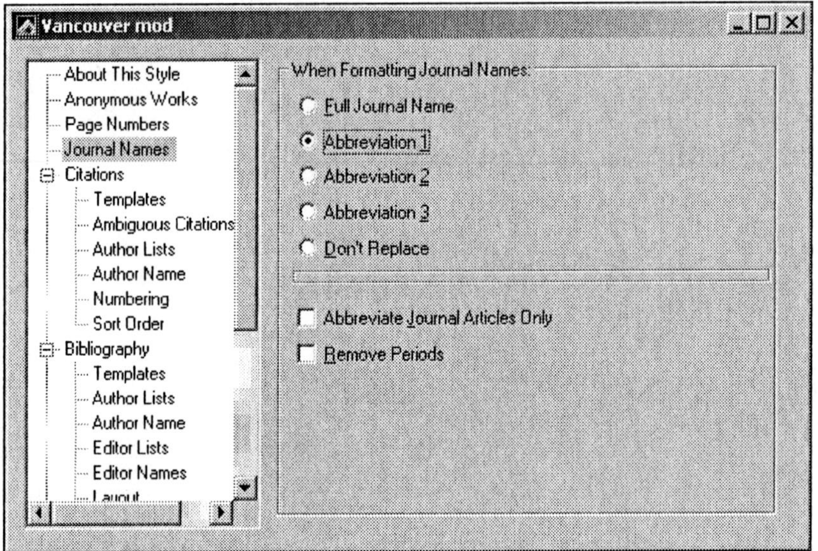

- **Follow These Steps**
  1. Open the Style.
  2. Choose **Journal Names**.
  3. Select the applicable option corresponding to the columns of the opened Journals Term List.
  4. Save settings.

Deleting the Issue number

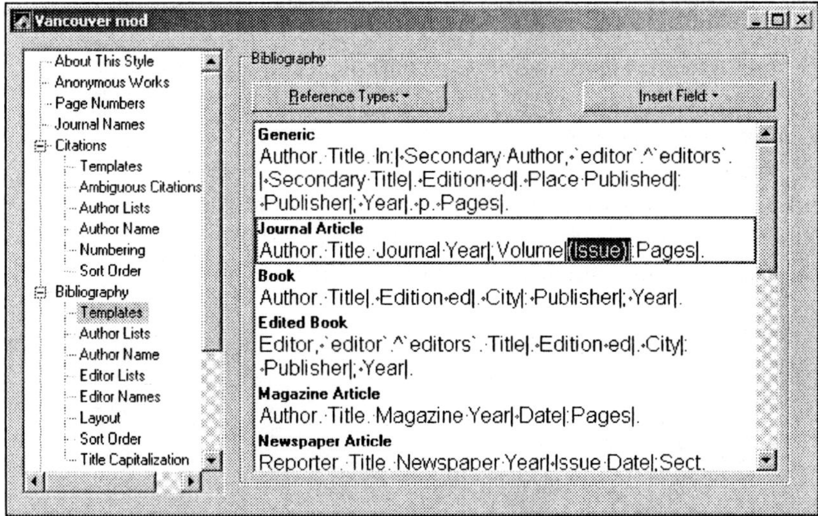

- **Follow These Steps**
  1. Open the Style.
  2. Choose **Bibliography - Templates**.
  3. Highlight *(Issue)|* in the Journal Article instruction box.
  4. Delete with **Edit - Clear** or the [**Del**]-key.
  5. Save settings.

Finally, in order to make these modifications have an effect on the citations and the bibliography in the manuscript, refresh is made with the normal Format Bibliography command.

Cited Pages

EndNote offers the possibility of using a special virtual field, Cited Pages, when creating a Style. The Cited Pages field can only be used in the Citation Template and the Footnote Template. This field may be used as if it was any other field. Text attributes may also be applied.

The information in this field however is not in the EndNote library, but it the Word document and individual for each citation. The Cited Pages information is inserted under the **Tools - EndNote α**[25] **- Edit Citation(s)** or [**Alt**] + [**6**]. See page 66.

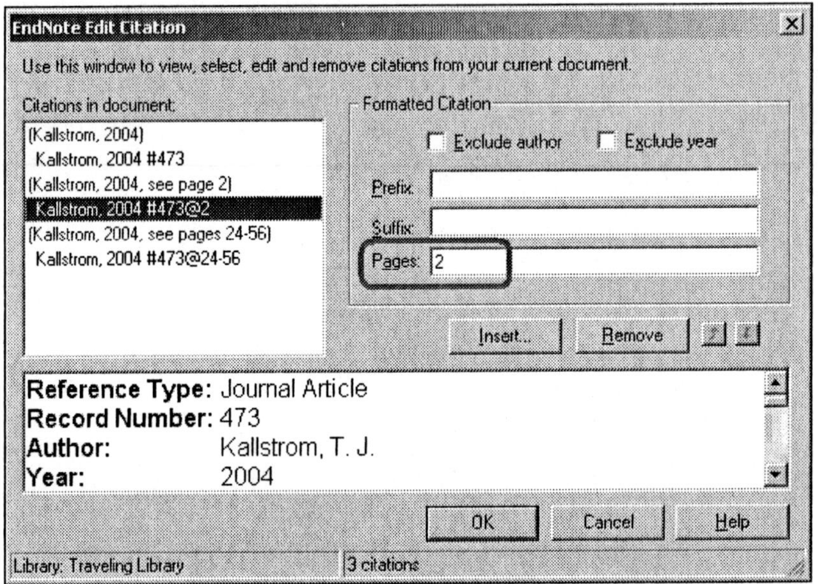

For example, let's assume we have the following instruction in the Citation Template of a particular Style:

```
(Author, Year|,°see°page^`pages`°Cited Pages)
```

Depending on what we type in the **Pages:** textbox we will have the following alternative results of a formatted in-text citation:

- Typed in the textbox **Pages:**
  - upon formatting: `(Kallstrom, 2004)`
- Typed in the textbox **Pages:** `2`
  - upon formatting: `(Kallstrom, 2004, see page 2)`
- Typed in the textbox Pages: `24-56`
  - upon formatting: `(Kallstrom, 2004, see pages 24-56)`

[25] Where α represents 7, 8, 9, or X depending on the EndNote-version.

Special Symbols used in Styles

With the previous example we list some comments on special symbols used in Styles:

- **|** Forced Separation (vertical bar) is used for unlinking elements in a template instruction. That means if a referred field is empty then linked or adjacent text elements will be omitted up to the Forced Separation character.
- **°** Link Adjacent text means that when a field is not empty then the adjacent text elements will display.
- **^** Singular/Plural between two text elements means that the first element is used when the singular applies and the second when the plural applies.
- **`** surrounding a word implies a text element in contrast to a field element should a confusion occur.
- **→** Tab
- **¶** End-of-Paragraph.

Testing a Modified Output Style

There are two ways to view the effect of a modified style on a record. It is quite normal to modify and view repeatedly before the required result is achieved.

The first preview option is already available in the library window. In the rightmost lower corner of the library window there is a **[Show Preview]**-button. A click on this button opens a new window and the text on button is changed to **[Hide Preview]**. This window displays the highlighted record formatted according to the current output style. Any saved modification of this style will have an immediate effect shown in this window.

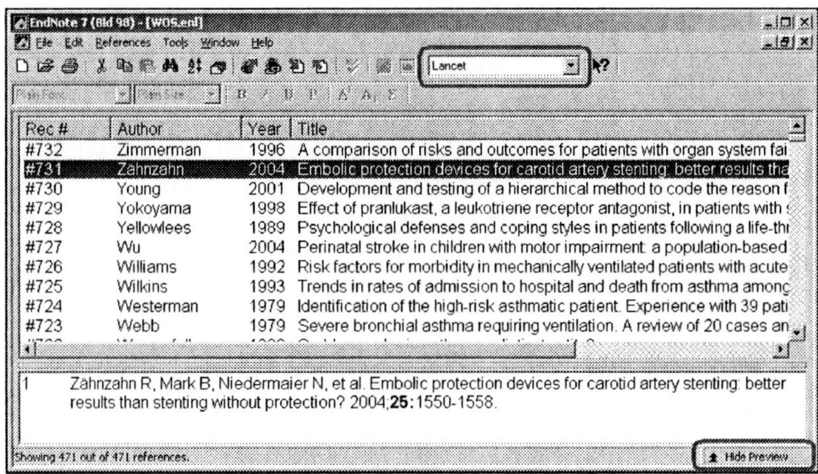

The Style Manager also has a preview function. Choose ***Style Preview*** from the drop-down list, highlight the style you need to examine and the result of three default references (the first is a Journal Article) are displayed in the lower window. The up and down arrows of the keyboard are used to scroll the list of styles.

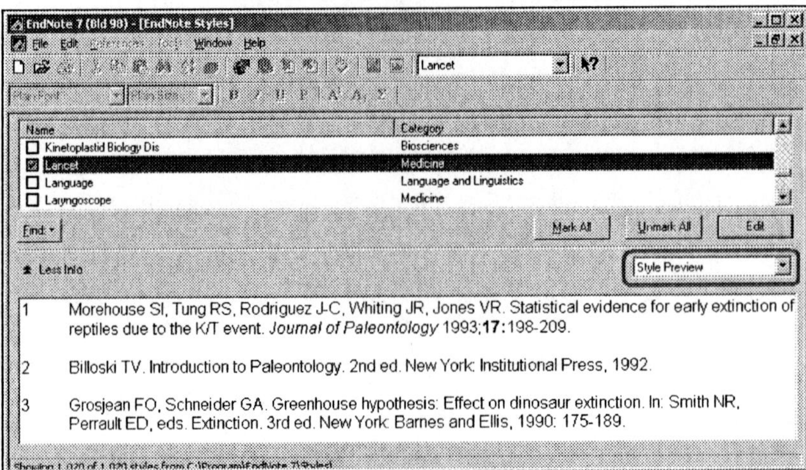

More on Indents, Margins, Tabs, and Text Attributes

This section is a result of frequently asked questions in connection with paragraph formatting of bibliographies. The section therefore takes up certain questions and the best suggested solutions.

Problem 1 – Too long a Tab Distance

This style requires no hanging indent but a tab after the bibliography number. The tab distance is far too long.

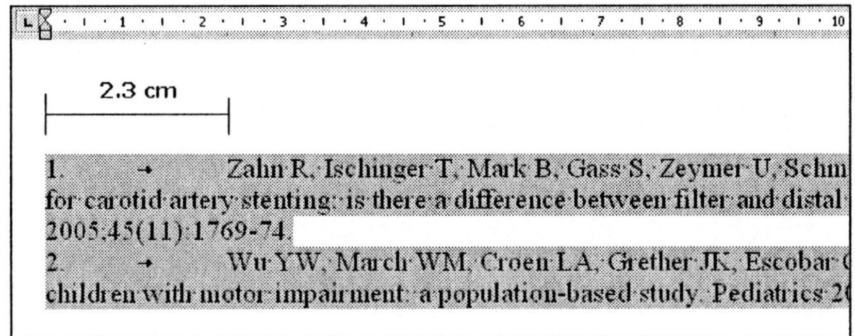

Solution: Word's default tab stops (usually 2.3 cm) is reflected in the paragraph formatting. To change (normally decrease) this distance go to Word: **Format - Tabs...**, select **Default tab stops:** *1 cm*. Confirm with **[OK]**. The modification will have an immediate effect.

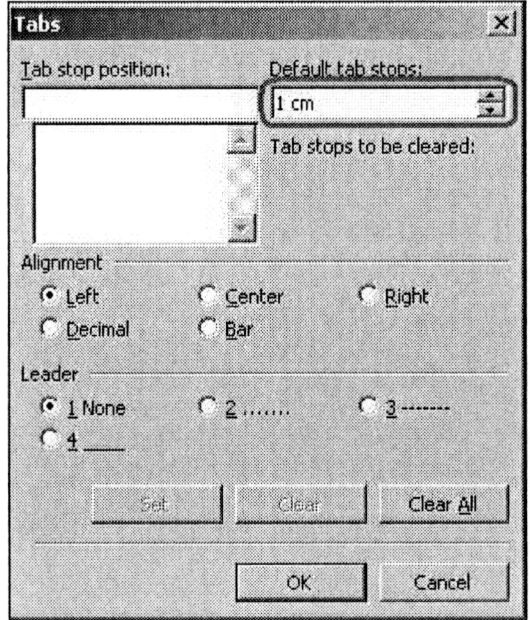

Problem 2 – A Tab precedes the Bibliography Number

This style requires no hanging indent but there is a tab before and a tab after the bibliography number. Both tab distances are far too long.

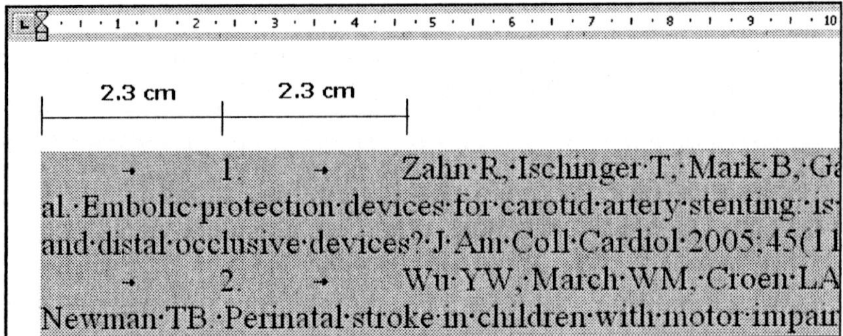

Solution: In EndNote, open the current style for editing, see page 75. Select the section **Bibliography – Layout,** delete the unwanted tab symbol, save the style, and refresh with the Format Bibliography command. Modify the standard distance for tabs according to the solution for Problem 1.

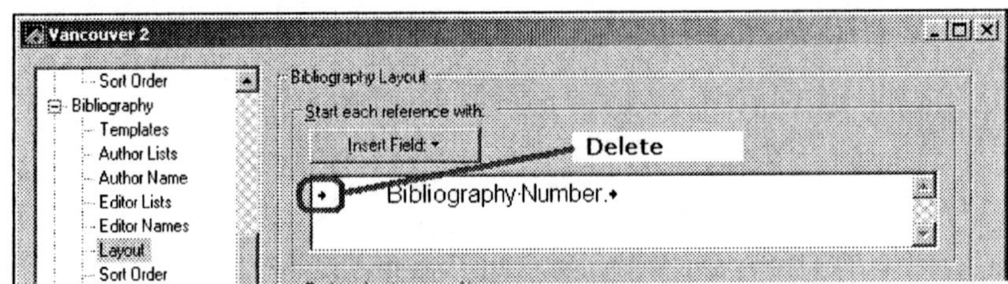

Problem 3 – Too long a Hanging Indent

This style has a hanging indent which is far too long.

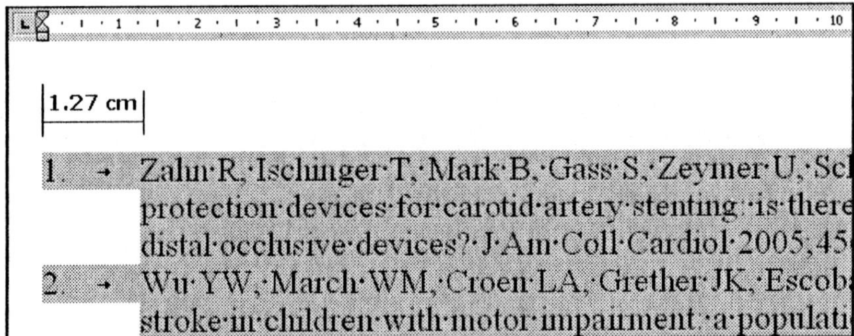

Solution: The standard distance for a hanging indent for new documents is 1.27 cm and is set in the dialog box **Format Bibliography**, the **Layout** tab and **Hanging indent.** Apply a new value, for example *0.8 cm* which will be saved for the current document. Confirm with **[OK]**.

Problem 4 – The Complete Bibliography is Bold

The complete bibliography is bold after formatting but only a few or none text elements according to the current style should be bold!

▪ REFERENCES¶
▪ ¶
▪ **1 → Zahn·R,·Mark·B,·Niedermaier·N,·et·al.·Embolic·protection·devices· for·carotid·artery·stenting:·better·results·than·stenting·without· protection?·2004;25:1550-1558.¶**

▪ **2 → Wu·YW,·March·WM,·Croen·LA,·Grether·JK,·Escobar·GJ,· Newman·TB.·Perinatal·stroke·in·children·with·motor·impairment:· a·population-based·study.·2004;114:612-619.¶**

Solution: When a bibliography is formatted for the first time the paragraph template from the last paragraph in the document applies but it uses fonts, size and tabs from paragraph template Normal. This implies that text attributes (bold, italic, superscript, subscript etc.) are inherited from this last paragraph. In other words if the last paragraph in the document is the title **REFERENCES** with attribute bold the whole bibliography will be bold the first time formatting is applied. If this is the case the whole bibliography must be unformatted with Unformat Citation(s). Then a new paragraph must be created with [**Enter**] and this new paragraph must be cleansed from all undesired attributes. Finally refresh with Format Bibliography.

About Footnotes

A Style determines how a footnote is formatted. In the open style mode **Footnotes - Templates** may be chosen. The prime choice is Format citations in footnotes: drop-down list. The options are:

- Same as Bibliography
- Same as In-Text Citations
- With Footnote Format

The two first options require no other settings other than the existing formatting instructions under the respective headings.

The third option, With Footnote Format, requires a complete formatting instruction in the Footnote Template textbox. The special field Cited Pages may be used, see page 82.

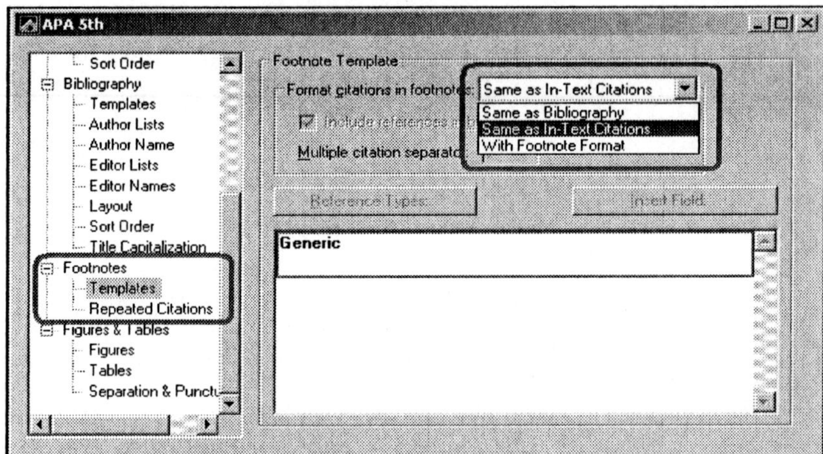

The section **Footnotes - Repeated Citations** offers settings for a short form of the repeated footnote. This is valid for all three options of the Footnote Template mentioned above. The short form includes only the Author names without initials. Title alt. Short Title can be added to the short form.

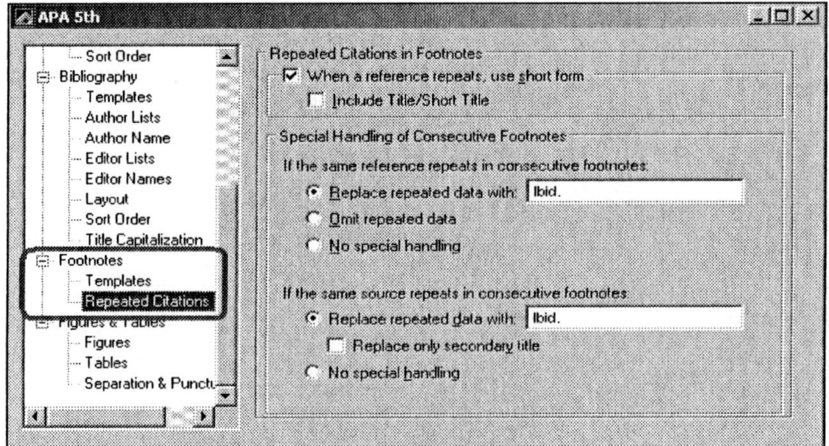

If the same reference or same source is repeated in consecutive footnotes there are detailed options on how to format the footnote citation.

15. REMOVING FIELD CODES

When you submit your paper to the publisher, the Word document must be formatted with the EndNote's Format Bibliography command. It is also highly recommended that the field codes be converted to text. If the field codes are left open in a computer that does not have EndNote, the document could easily be corrupted or be difficult to import by the publisher's word processor.

♦ **Follow These Steps**

1 Go to **Tools - EndNote α**[26] **- Remove Field Codes** or the icon .

EndNote will remind you to save the *Working Copy* and creates a new copy of the document where the field codes from EndNote have been converted to normal text. This copy of the document is usually referred to as *Publisher's Copy*. After the Remove Field Codes command you will need to save the new copy with a new name with the **Save As...** command. This copy cannot be restored for further EndNote editing. In case you need to edit your manuscript you must return to the Working Copy.

Field shading according to recommended settings on page 19 will make it easier during the working session to immediately recognize the Working Copy and Publisher's Copy respectively.

The working copy, formatted and with field shading:

Text text text text. (1) Text text text text. Text text text text. Text text text text. Text text text text. Text text text text. Text text text text. Text text text text. Text text text text. Text text text text. Text text text text. Text text text text. Text text text text. Text text text text. Text text text text. (2) Text text text text. Text text text text. Text text text text. (3) Text text text text. Text text text text. Text text text text. Text text text text. Text text text text.¶

¶

REFERENCES¶

¶

1. → Ververeli K, Chipps B. Oral corticosteroid-sparing effects of inhaled corticosteroids in the treatment of persistent and acute asthma. Ann Allergy Asthma Immunol 2004;92(5):512-22.¶

2. → Kallstrom TJ. Evidence-based asthma management. Respir Care 2004;49(7):783-92.¶

3. → Patel PH, Welsh C, Foggs MB. Improved asthma outcomes using a coordinated care approach in a large medical group. Dis Manag 2004;7(2):102-11.¶

The publisher's copy with field codes converted to text:

Text text text text. (1) Text text text text. Text text text text. Text text text text. Text text text text. Text text text text. Text text text text. Text text text text. Text text text text. Text text text text. Text text text text. Text text text text. Text text text text. Text text text text. Text text text text. (2) Text text text text. Text text text text. Text text text text. (3) Text text text text. Text text text text. Text text text text. Text text text text. Text text text text.¶

¶

REFERENCES¶

¶

1. → Ververeli K, Chipps B. Oral corticosteroid-sparing effects of inhaled corticosteroids in the treatment of persistent and acute asthma. Ann Allergy Asthma Immunol 2004;92(5):512-22.¶

2. → Kallstrom TJ. Evidence-based asthma management. Respir Care 2004;49(7):783-92.¶

3. → Patel PH, Welsh C, Foggs MB. Improved asthma outcomes using a coordinated care approach in a large medical group. Dis Manag 2004;7(2):102-11.¶

[26] Where α represents 7, 8, 9, or X depending on the EndNote-version.

Manually Removing Field Codes

Word's generic command for removing field codes, **[Ctrl]** + **[6]**, may at certain occasions be an alternative method.

- **Follow These Steps**
  1. Highlight the fields you want to unlink, or if all text, then use key command **[Ctrl]** + **[A]**.
  2. Unlink with key command **[Ctrl]** + **[6]**.
  3. Go to **File - Save As...** and determine name and file location of your unlinked document.

This is the preferred procedure when using the EndNote's Word templates as described in Chapter 18, page 105.

A few important considerations specific for this method are:

- If your document contains *footnotes* with field codes that you want to unlink, then you need to highlight the document body and the footnote window separately and do the unlinking for each window.
- Unlinking a whole document with this method removes *all field codes* even such field codes that are not created by EndNote, for example cross references, tables of contents, indexes etc.
- Embedded or linked objects like objects from Excel Worksheets or Charts applying layout mode *In line with text* will be unlinked and converted to Picture objects (Windows Metafile) which is the preferred format when sending a manuscript to a publisher.

16. TERM LISTS

EndNote has the capacity to create term lists built up from certain field(s) and related to an individual library. Term lists are alphabetically sorted lists with eliminated duplicates. EndNote is by default prepared to create term lists for Authors, Keywords, and Journals. Term Lists can also be imported from external sources and exported as textfiles for use in other applications.

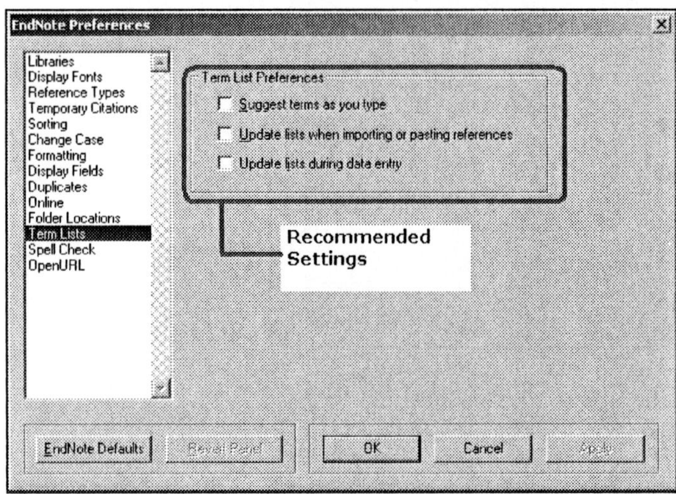

By factory default Term Lists Preferences are set for suggesting terms and automatic update. We recommend however, that the preferences are set for manual handling of term lists.

- **Follow These Steps**
  1. Go to **Edit - Preferences**.
  2. Choose section **Term Lists**.
  3. Uncheck all three options.
  4. Confirm with **[OK]**.

The reason why we recommend manual update of term lists is that term lists can unnecessarily oversize the libraries for those who do not use term lists. Also automatic update does not reduce term lists when records are deleted, which may cause term lists to grow out of control.

Term lists have import and export options.

A term list of special significance is the Journals Term List, which has four columns with alternative terms, or synonyms.

Creating a New Term List

In certain circumstances there is a need for special term lists, e.g. for chemicals and substances.

♦ **Follow These Steps**

1 Open the EndNote library for which you need the term list.

2 Go to **Tools - Define Term Lists...**
or key command **[Ctrl]** + [**4**].

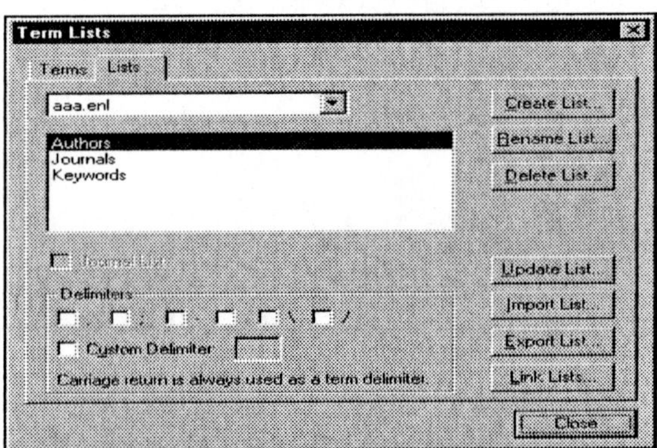

3 Use the [**Create List...**]-button.

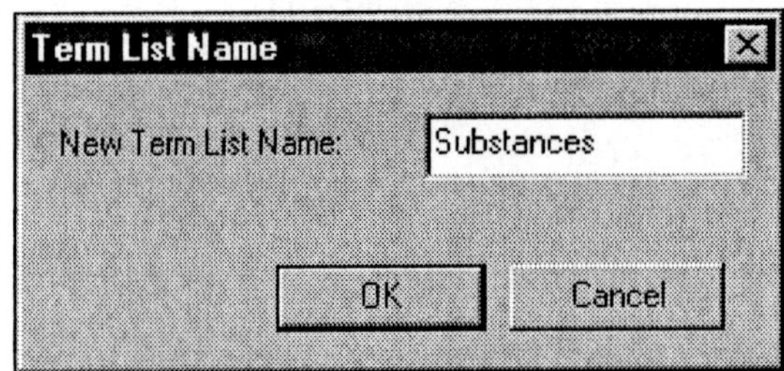

4 Type a new name for the new term list, e.g. `Substances`.

5 Confirm with [**OK**] followed by [**OK**] in the Term Lists-window.

Linking the Term List to Certain Fields

1 Go to **Tools - Link Term Lists...**
or key command **[Ctrl]** + [**3**].

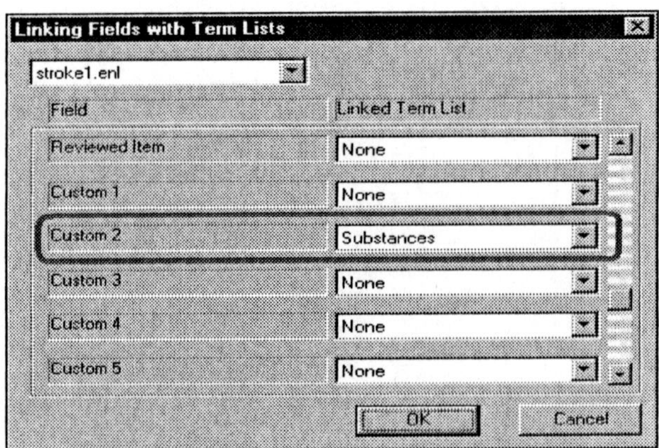

2 Scroll the list until the field **Custom 2** is shown in the left column.
3 Select a term list, *Substances*, from the drop-down list in the right column. If required, more than one field can be linked to a term list.
4 Confirm with **[OK]**.

Manual Update of Term List

We suggest the manual update of term lists. To ensure that the term list only accommodates terms from existing records the list needs to be set to zero and then updated.

♦ **Follow These Steps**

1 Open the term list.
2 Select all terms with key command **[Ctrl]** + **[A]**.
3 Delete all terms with the **[Delete Term]**-button.
4 Update with the **[Update List...]**-button from the **Lists** tab.

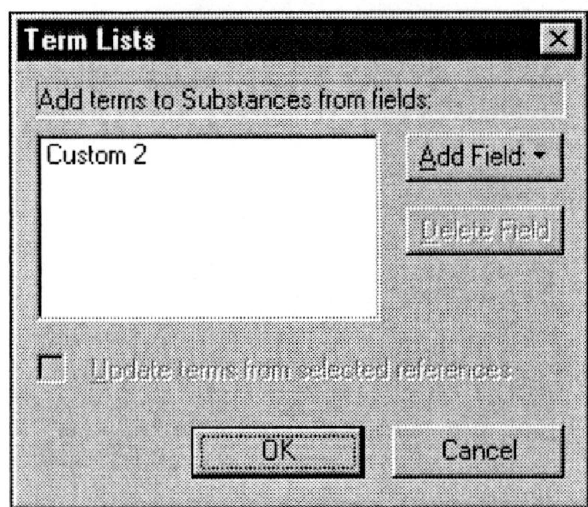

5 Confirm with **[OK]**.

Opening Term List

All term lists are accessible under **Tools** - **Open Term Lists**. It is convenient to select the name of the term list with the pointer.

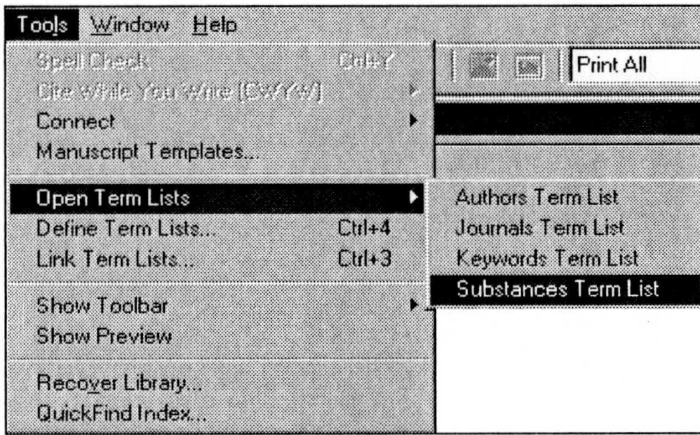

The term list will open:

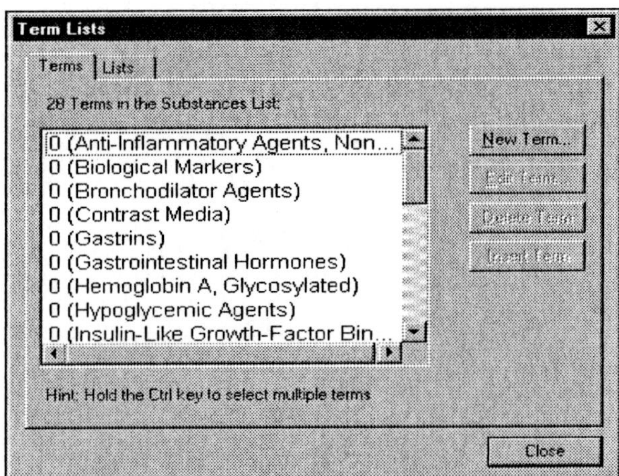

Importing Term Lists

When there is a need to use synonyms or alternative journal names an external term list may be imported. Please note, that the Journal Term List is a four column list prepared for a set of synonyms per row.

- **Follow These Steps**
  1. Go to **Tools - Open Term Lists.**
  2. Select **Journals Term List**.
  3. Use the **Terms** tab and highlight all terms with **[Ctrl]** + **[A]**.
  4. Delete all terms with the **[Delete Term]**-button.
  5. Use the **List** tab and highlight **Journals**.
  6. Click the **[Import List...]**-button.
  7. Select appropriate Term List such as one residing in the Term Lists folder.
  8. Confirm with **[Open]**.

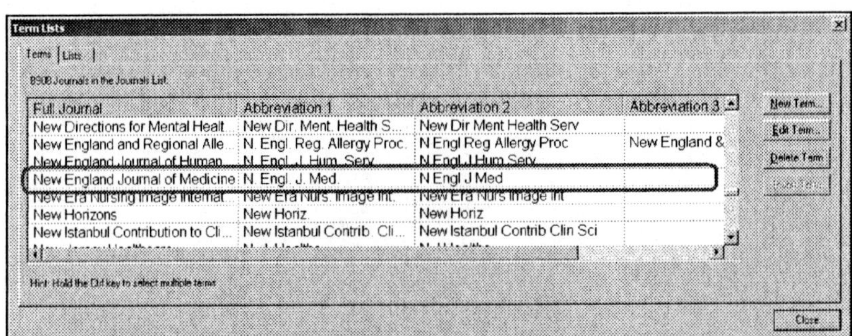

9. Close with **[Close]**.

This option should be used only when needed and in combination with Styles set for alternative journal names. See page 80. Please also note, that such term lists are specific for each library. If several libraries are used for Styles set for alternative journal names then each library must import such term lists. Large term lists makes the size of each library grow and should therefore not be used unless really needed.

Searching with Term Lists

- **Follow These Steps**

1 Go to **References - Search References...**
or key command **[Ctrl]** + **[F]**
or the icon
or right-click the mouse and select **Search References...**
and the search form will display.

2 Select the *Custom 2* field and place the cursor in the textbox.

3 Use key command **[Ctrl]** + **[1]** and the linked term list will automatically open.

4 Highlight a term with the pointer or type the initial character (or, typing quickly, the two or even three initial characters) of the wanted term, which will then be highlighted.

5 Double-click the term or apply **[Insert Term]** and the term will be pasted into the textbox.

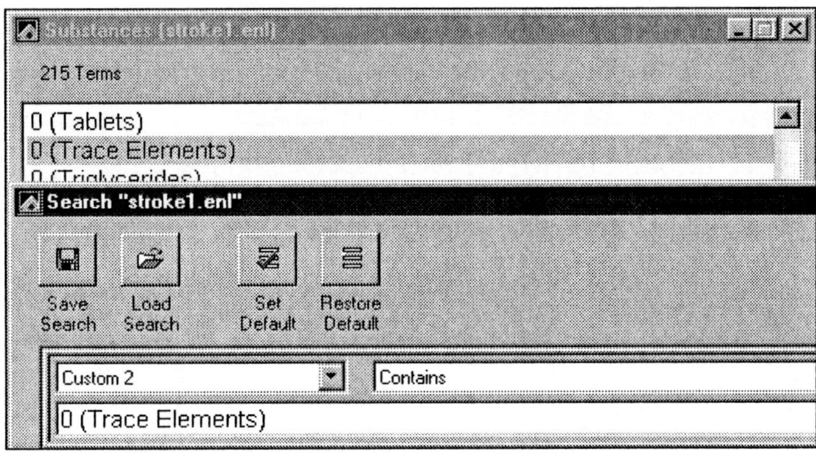

6 When required, add more terms or search strings in the forthcoming text boxes of the search form.

7 Click the **[Search]**-button or simply the **[Enter]**-key.

Creating Records with Term Lists

- **Follow These Steps**

1 Create a new reference with **References - New Reference**
or key command **[Alt]** + **[N]**
or the icon
or right-click the mouse and select **New Reference**
and the empty New reference window will display.

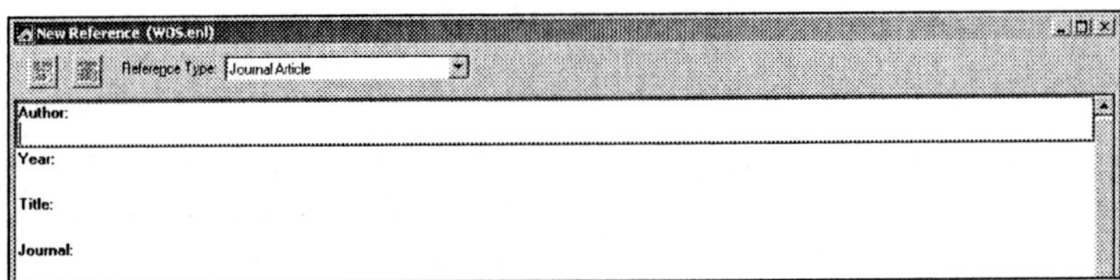

2 Position the cursor in the Author field.
3 Use key command **[Ctrl]** + [1] and the linked term list (Author) will open automatically.

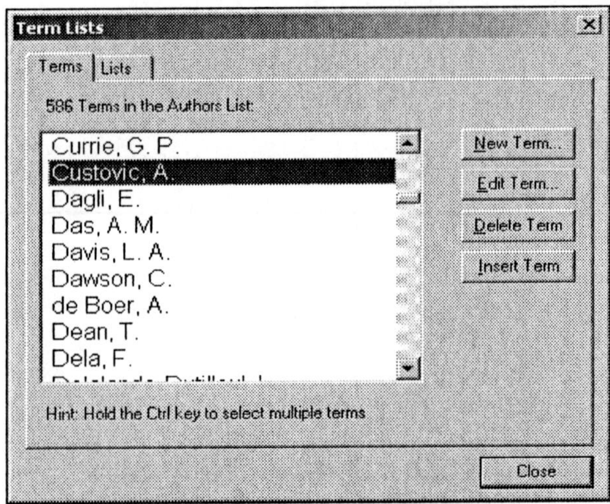

4 Highlight the term(s) you intend to insert and double-click or apply **[Insert Term]**.

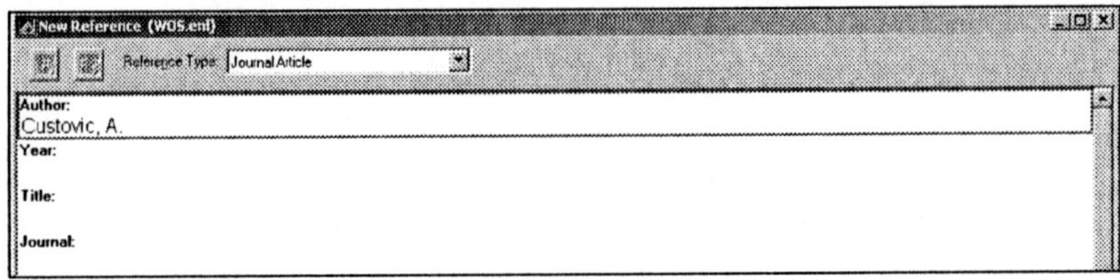

You may then proceed to other linked fields and apply the same procedure.

17. DATABASE PRODUCTION TOOLS

EndNote has the capacity of not only to import and capture data from external databases but also to build databases of its own. This will be necessary for many users who need references for manuscript writing but do not have access to databases with convenient data transfer capacity to reference handling software.

There are also many occasions when data imported or captured from external sources will need some cleaning up due to imperfections in original data or import procedures.

In some cases third party software like Microsoft Excel or FileMaker may be of valuable assistance for the production of databases. In those cases a tab delimited textfile is often the format that makes data transfer between EndNote and a third party software possible.

Exporting Data - General

The export function in EndNote is characterized by the following:

- Exported references are the currently viewed records
- The current Output Style determines the structure of the file
- File formats options are textfile, RTF, HTML, XML

♦ **Follow These Steps**

1 Activate the current library.

2 Select a suitable Output Style, e.g. *Tab Delimited.*

3 If all records in the library will be exported apply **References - Show All References** and proceed to 5 otherwise highlight the records you intend to export.

4 Go to **References - Show Selected References**.

5 Go to **File - Export...**

6 Determine name and file location and file format e.g. text file.

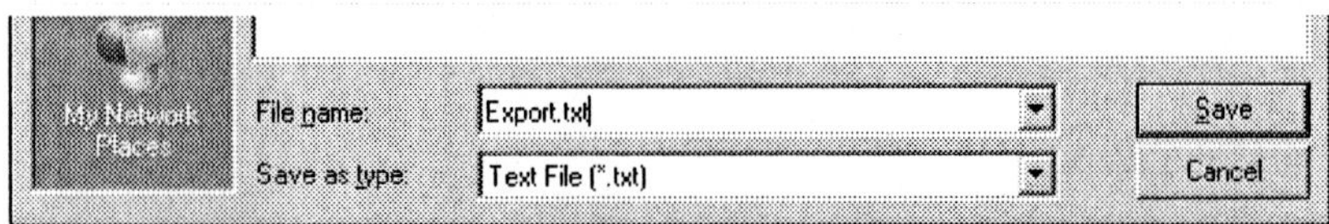

7 Confirm with **[Save]**.

The exported data can now be imported by third party software that can import tab-delimited textfiles. Note however, that a tab-delimited EndNote export file can not be re-imported to EndNote unless it is restructured in compliance with the requirements on page 99.

Exporting Data to Excel

When the need arises to export data to Excel for restructuring or modification some special considerations are necessary.

♦ **Follow These Steps**

1. Activate the current library.
2. Select the special Output Style, *Tab Delimited EN7 Excel.ens*[27] if you use EndNote 7 or earlier, *Tab Delimited EN8 Excel.ens*[27] if you use EndNote 8 or later.
3. Replace all line feeds in the library with semicolon using **Edit - Change Text...** and type **Search for: [Ctrl]** + **[Enter]**[28] and **Change the text to: ;** **[Space]**.

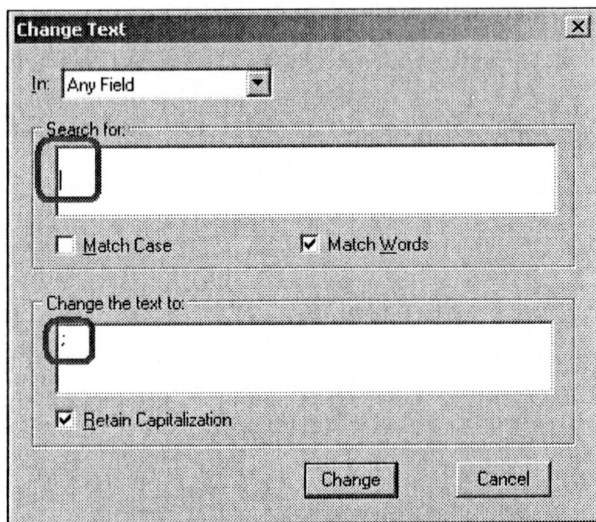

4. Confirm with **[Change]**.
5. Highlight the references you want to export. If you want to export the whole library, use key command for Show All **[Ctrl]** + **[M]** then for Highlight All **[Ctrl]** + **[A]**.
6. Use key command for Copy Formatted, **[Ctrl]** + **[K]**.
7. Open Excel and click on the *General Templates* option in the Activity Window. Under the **EndNote** tab, select the template *EndNote7.xlt*[27] if you use EndNote 7 or earlier, *EndNote8.xlt*[27] if you use EndNote 8 or later. If this tab does not appear, please read the instructions on page 105. (This template has been designed so that all EndNote generic fields are already typed on **Row 1** of the spreadsheet according to the requirements below.)
8. Place the cursor in **Cell A2** of the Excel worksheet and paste the contents of the clipboard with **[Ctrl]** + **[V]**.
9. You may now modify your data but keep Row 1 with the EndNote field names intact.
10. Save the worksheet as an Excel worksheet, *.xls.

[27] The Excel Templates may be downloaded from the Author's website according to instructions at the end of this book.

[28] EndNote 9 carries an imperfection so that this command does not work.

Importing Tab Delimited Data - General

A tab delimited textfile that can be imported by EndNote must be structured in one of the following two ways:

a) If same reference types apply to all records then the file may have the following structure:

(^p means line feed and ^t means tab; the field names in the second line are the field names from reference type Generic or from the reference type that will be imported; exact spelling of field names is necessary, all fields must not be present, order between the columns is not critical, empty columns must not exist to the left of the last column.)

```
*Journal Article^p
Author^t      Year^t        Title^t       Journal^t     Volume^t      Etc.^p
<field1>^t    <field2>^t    <field3>^t    <field4>^t    <field5>^t    Etc.^p
<field1>^t    <field2>^t    <field3>^t    <field4>^t    <field5>^t    Etc.^p
```

b) If various reference types apply to the records then the file must have the following structure:

(The field names must be from reference type Generic; exact spelling of field names is necessary, all fields must not be present, order between the columns is not critical, empty columns must not exist to the left of the last column.)

```
Reference Type^t    Author^t    Year^t      Title^t     Secondary Title^t Etc.^p
Journal Article ^t  <field1>^t  <field2>^t  <field3>^t  <field4>^t        Etc.^p
Book^t              <field1>^t  <field2>^t  <field3>^t  <field4>^t        Etc.^p
```

Any textfile that follows the described structures can be imported by EndNote.

♦ **Follow These Steps**

1 Activate the current library.

2 Go to **File - Import...**

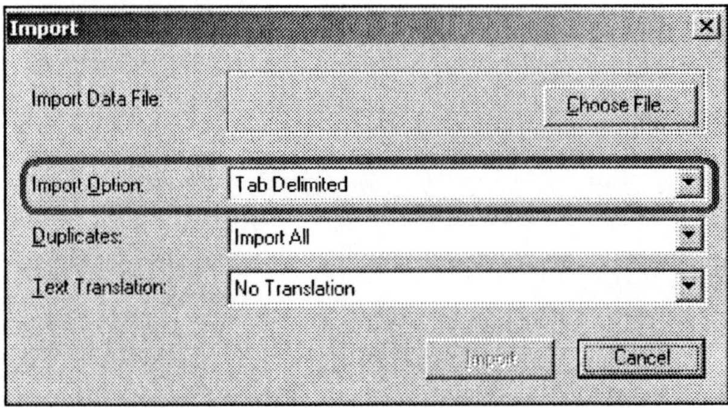

3 Use the **[Choose File...]**-button to browse and find the structured textfile.

4 Select *Tab Delimited* from the **Import Option** drop-down list.

5 Confirm with **[Import]**.

Importing Data from Excel

- **Follow These Steps**
  1. Open the specially structured Excel worksheet described in previous section.
  2. Select all text with **[Ctrl]** + **[A]**.
  3. Copy the whole document with **[Ctrl]** + **[C]**.
  4. Create a new document in Microsoft Notes.
  5. Paste with **[Ctrl]** + **[V]**.
  6. Go to **File** - **Save As...** and determine name file location of the textfile.
  7. Create a new or open an existing EndNote library.
  8. Go to **File** - **Import...**
  9. Use the **[Choose File...]**-button to browse and find the structured textfile.
  10. Select *Tab Delimited* from the **Import Option** drop-down list.
  11. Confirm with **[Import]**.
  12. Replace all semicolons plus space in the library with line feeds using **Edit** - **Change Text...** and type **Search for: ; [Space]** and **Change the text to: [Ctrl]** + **[Enter]**[29].

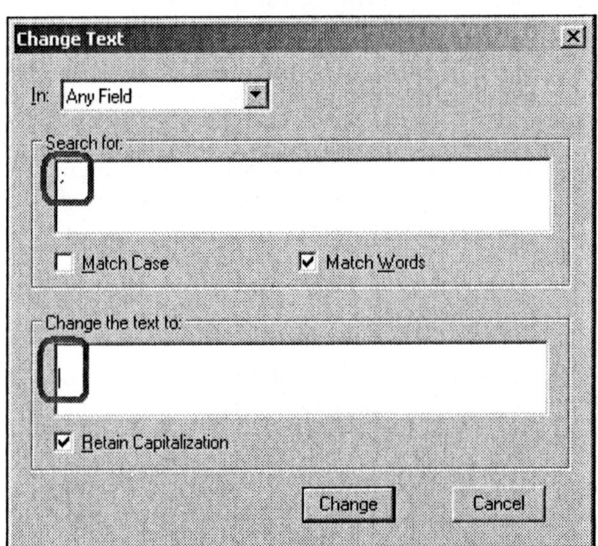

  13. Confirm with **[Change]**.

[29] EndNote 9 carries an imperfection so that this command does not work.

Spell Check

EndNote has a built in Spellchecker, which operates on an individual record level.

- **Follow These Steps**
  1. Activate the current library.
  2. Open the record(s) you wish to spell-check.
  3. Go to **Tools - Spell Check**
     or key command **[Ctrl]** + **[Y]**.

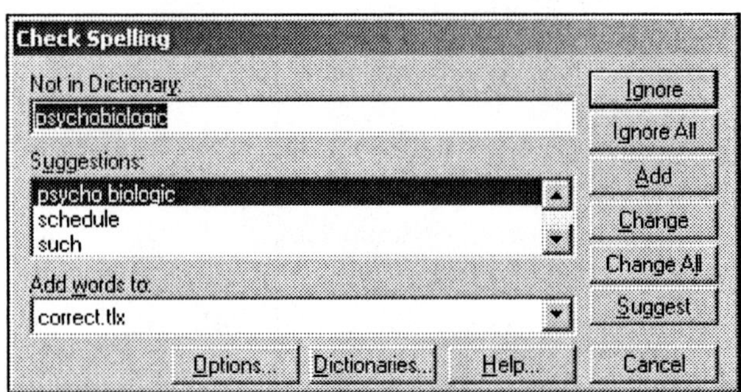

[**Ignore**] means that the word found not to be in the dictionary would be left unchanged

[**Ignore All**] means that all occurrences of the found word will be left unchanged

[**Add**] means that the word found would be added to the current dictionary displayed in the Add words to: box

[**Change**] means that the found word will be replaced by the suggested replacement

[**Change All**] means that all occurrences of the found word will be replaced by the suggested replacement

[**Suggest**] means that a deeper search for replacement is made until the button is disabled

[**Options**] determines the choice of Main Dictionary language and a number of other options

[**Dictionaries**] determines what dictionaries are used in addition to the Main Dictionary selected under Options above

The Options and Dictionaries reflect settings made under **Edit - Preferences - Spell Check**, see page 17.

Spell Check Options:

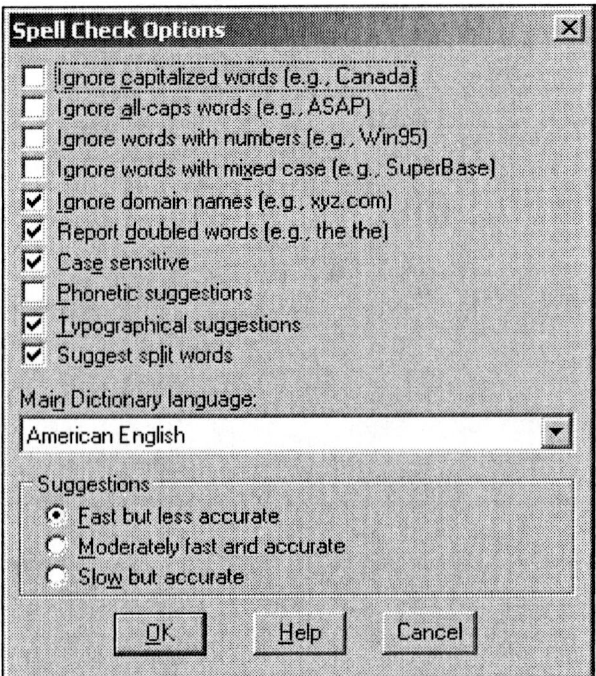

Dictionaries:

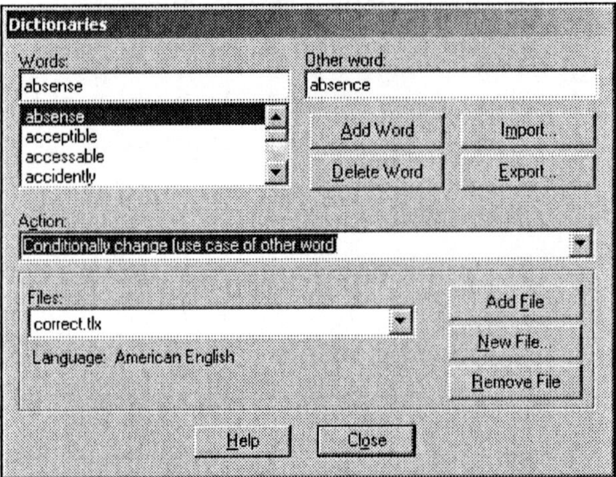

The selected dictionaries are listed in the drop-down list under **Files:**. Existing dictionaries can be added with the [**Add File**]-button or removed with the [**Remove File**]-button.

Under **Words:** are listed such misspelled or other words that should be replaced by words listed under **Other word:**

Here you may add words or terms and its suggested replacement. For each such Word a specific action (6 options) is chosen from the drop-down list. Changes are saved with the [**Add Word**]-button. Words can be deleted with the [**Delete Word**]-button.

Changing Text

Any text in a library can be changed or deleted in selected records.

♦ **Follow These Steps**

1. Activate the current library.
2. If all records in the library will be subject to change(s) apply **References - Show All References** and proceed to 4 otherwise highlight the records you intend to change.
3. Go to **References - Show Selected References**.
4. Go to **Edit - Change Text...** or **[Ctrl]** + **[R]**.

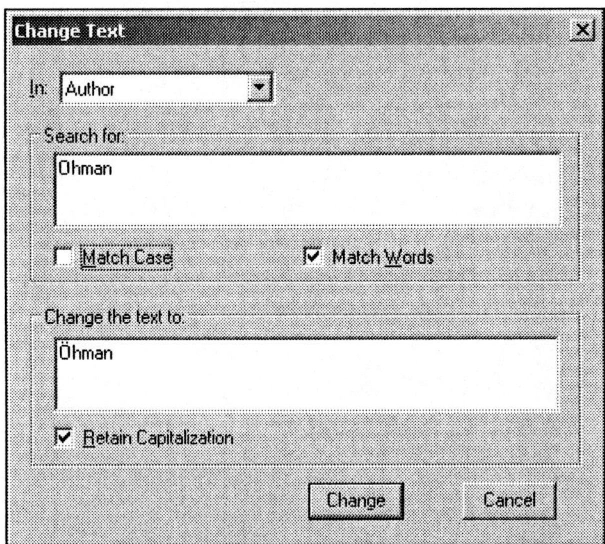

5. Select a field in the drop-down list under **In**: Type the **Search for** text and the **Change to** text.
6. Apply with **[Change]**.

Changing and Moving Fields

Whole fields can be added, replaced, deleted, or moved in selected records.

♦ **Follow These Steps**

1. Activate the current library.
2. If all records in the library will be subject to change(s) apply **References - Show All References** and proceed to 4 otherwise highlight the records you intend to change.
3. Go to **References - Show Selected References**.
4. Go to **References - Change and Move Fields...**

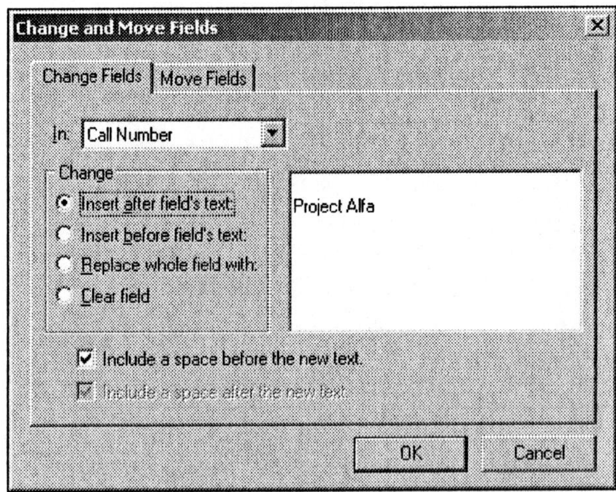

5 In the **Change Fields** tab select the field that shall be modified from the drop-down list.
6 Select **Change** option and type the new text in the text box. If you need to type (or start with) line feed use **[Ctrl]** + **[Enter]**[30].
7 Apply with **[OK]**.

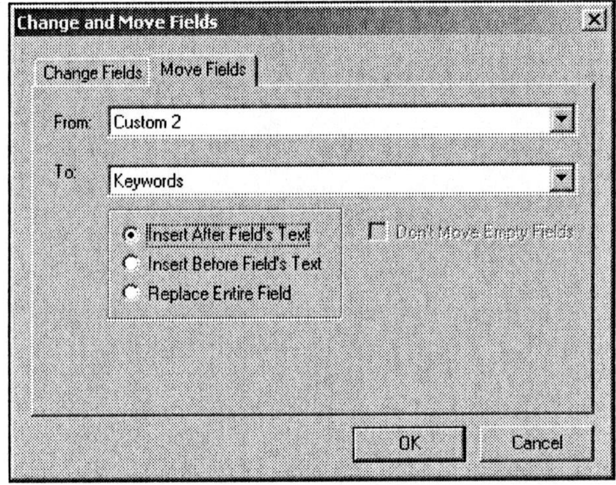

8 In the **Move Fields** tab select the From field and the To field from the drop-down lists.
9 Select applicable option.
10 Apply with **[OK]**.

[30] EndNote 9 carries an imperfection so that this command does not work.

18. MANUSCRIPT TEMPLATES

EndNote includes a large collection of Word Templates that represent a more comprehensive interpretation of author instructions than only how to handle references. These templates incorporate various macros and other help functions for the benefit of scientific writers.

The templates are named after the journals for which they are designed, as they do with the styles. With these templates many formatting issues are already set up for your target publication, such as proper margins, headings, pagination, line spacing, title page, abstract page, graphics placement, and font type, and size. The use of templates can be initiated from either EndNote or Word.

Installing an Endnote-Tab for Templates in Word and Excel

Normally you need to install manually the EndNote-tab for templates in Word which makes it easier to find EndNote's Word templates. This EndNote-tab will also be available within Excel for EndNote's Excel templates should such templates exist.

Should the EndNote-tab already exist then proceed to next section.

♦ **Follow These Steps**

1. Open *Windows Explorer.*
2. Open your EndNote installation folder, normally C:\Program Files\EndNote\.
3. Highlight the EndNote subfolder *Templates.*

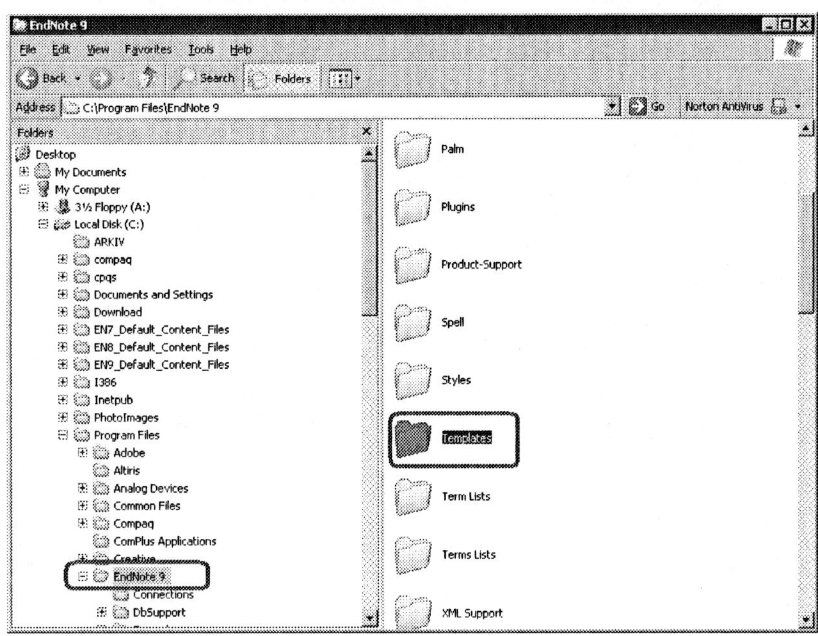

4. Go to **Edit - Copy**
   or key command **[Ctrl]** + **[C]**
   or right-click the mouse and select **Copy**.

5 Open your Microsoft Templates folder, normally C:\Documents and Settings\<username>\Application Data\Microsoft\Templates.
6 Highlight the Microsoft subfolder *Templates*.
7 Go to **Edit - Paste Shortcut**.
8 The shortcut icon created must be renamed to *EndNote*. Highlight the shortcut icon, go to **File** - **Rename** or right-click the mouse and select **Rename** and type `EndNote`. Confirm with **[Enter]**

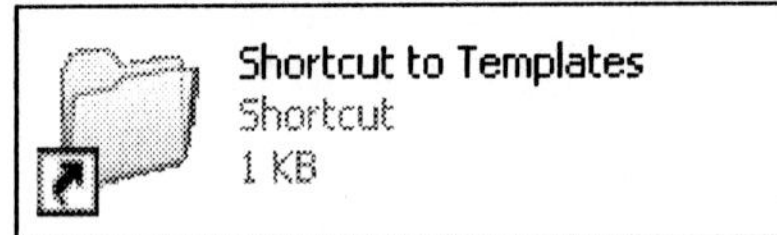

9 Open Word.
10 Go to **File - New...**
11 Click on the **On my computer...** option in the **Task Pane**.

The **EndNote** tab is now available in the **Templates** dialog box:

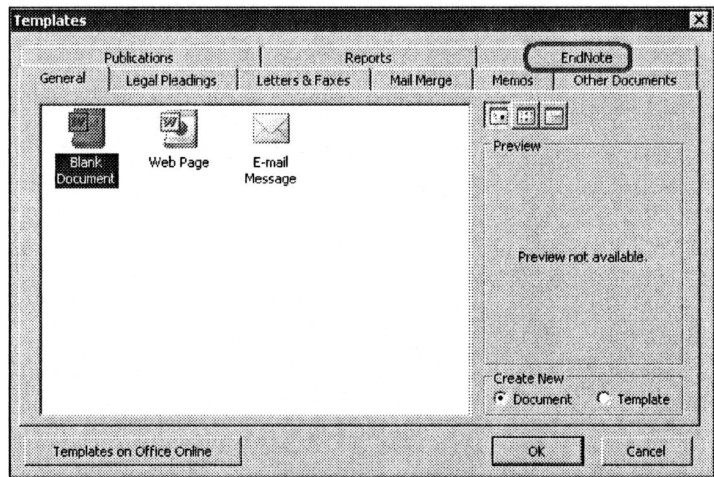

12 Click on the **EndNote** tab and all templates that were installed when EndNote was installed are available for selection.

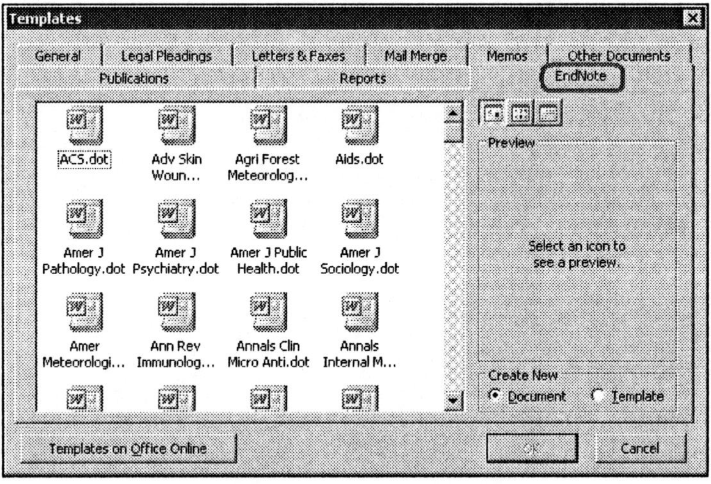

If you want to change the view of the list of templates, use one of the view buttons for instance the Detailed View option:

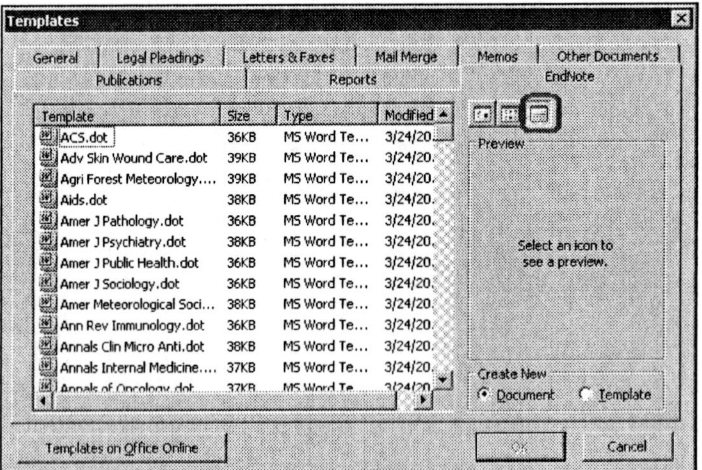

From here you can simply highlight a template and then click on **[OK]**.

Using Word Templates

From EndNote:

♦ **Follow These Steps**

1 Go to **Tools - Manuscript Templates.**

2 Choose a template and confirm with **[Open]**.

From Word:

♦ **Follow These Steps**

1 Go to **File - New...**

2 Click on the **On my computer...** option on the **Task Pane**.

The **EndNote** tab is now visible in the **Templates** dialog box, if not, see previous section:

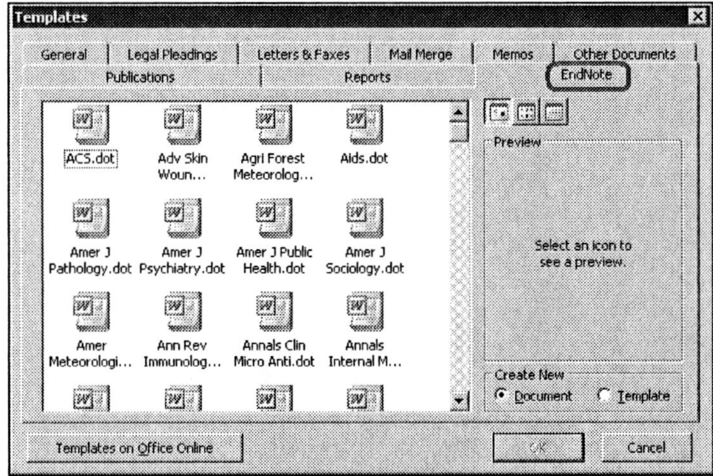

3 Choose a template and confirm with **[OK]**.

When a template has been chosen and a new Word document has been created and the following message displays:

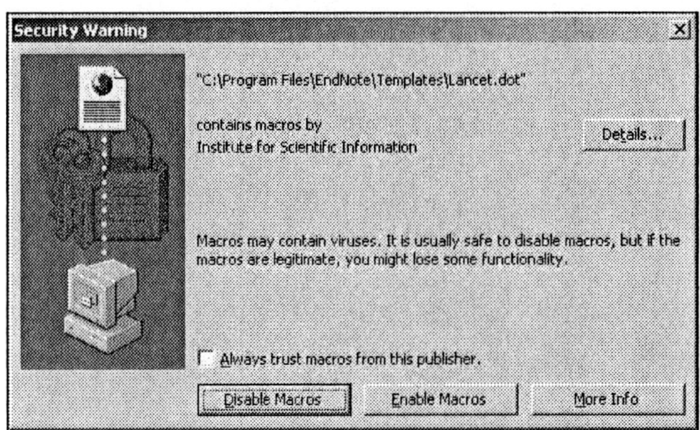

4 Since the template collection is based on the use of macros you need to accept with the **[Enable Macros]**-button.

A Wizard will lead you through the most important sections of the document such as Title, Author names, Keywords etc. We exemplify with the Template and Wizard for Lancet:

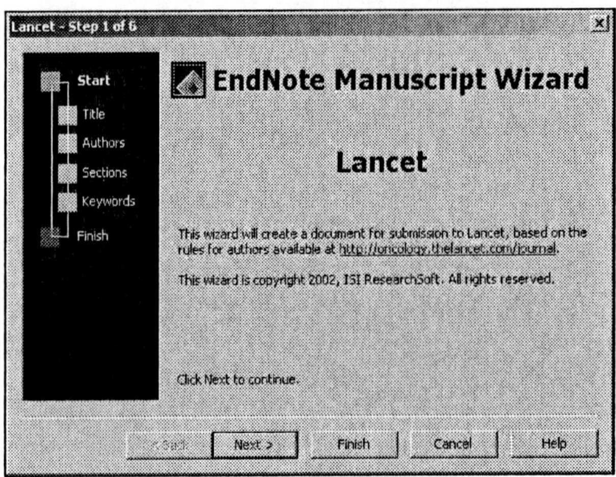

5 Click on [**Next** >].

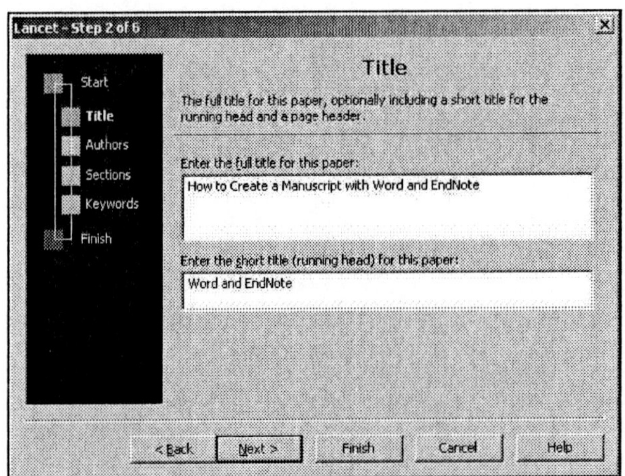

6 Fill in the textboxes for the full title and the short title. Click on [**Next** >].

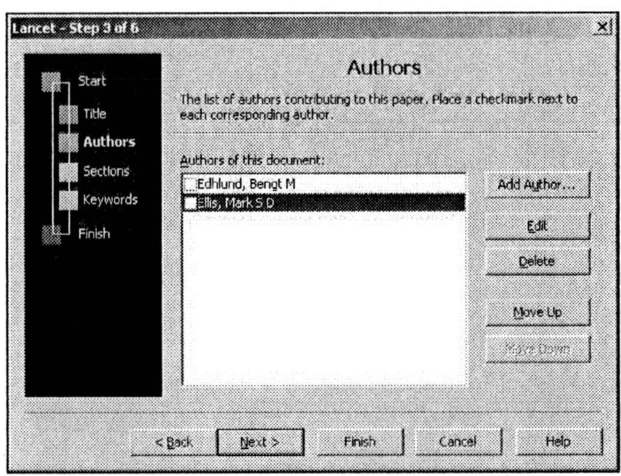

7 Author names and address information can be captured from the [**Add Author**]-button, which also makes it possible to connect to Outlook and your address book. Once authors are listed in your templates they can easily be added when you create new manuscripts. Click on [**Next** >].

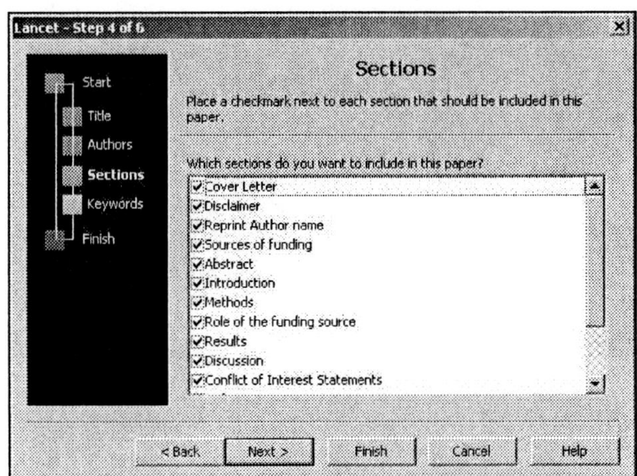

8 You can easily select which sections you want to use in your manuscript. Click on [**Next** >].

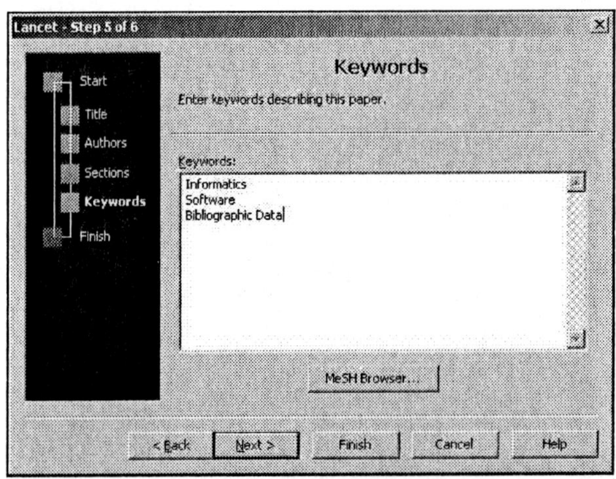

9 The publishers often require a listing of keywords from the authors. To facilitate the use of Medical Subheadings, MeSH, the button **[MeSH-Browser...]** links directly to the MeSH-browser on the Web at National Library of Medicine, NLM. The final indexing as applied in PubMed is however in the hands of NLM. Click on **[Next** >].

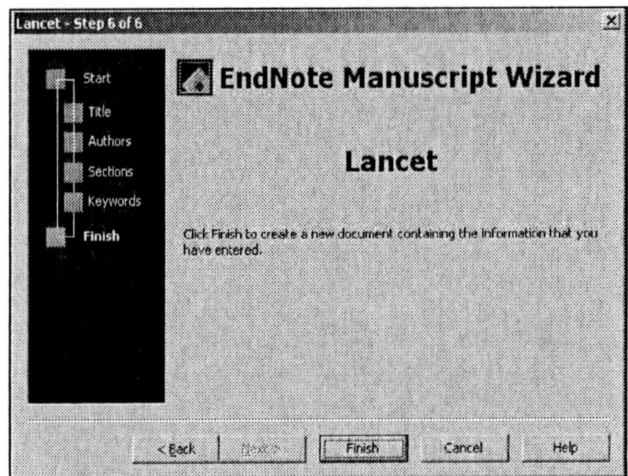

10 Click on **[Finish]**.

A document created this way also includes all necessary CWYW-settings as dealt with in Chapter 9, page 51. This includes the selection of Output Style; i.e. the Lancet style has already been selected. In case you would need some other Style, simply change before formatting takes place.

All data that we have submitted is now inserted in the Word document. Other data can be filled in on its respective places. Where there is a tag like:

`[Insert Methods here]`

You simply select this tag and overwrite it as you type.

[Insert·Title·of·Article]¶

[Insert·Names·of·Author(s)]¶

[Insert·Affiliation·information·here]¶

[Insert·Disclaimer·here]¶

[Insert·Corresponding·Author·information·here]¶

[Insert·Reprint·Author·name·here]¶

[Insert·Sources·of·funding·here]¶

[Insert·Running·Title·<40·characters]¶

Introduction¶

[Insert·Introduction·text·here]¶

Methods¶

[Insert·Methods·here]¶

Role·of·the·funding·source¶

[Insert·Role·of·the·funding·source·here]¶

Results¶

[Insert·Results]¶

Discussion¶

[Insert·Discussion·here]¶

Conflict·of·Interest·Statements¶

[Insert·Conflict·of·Interest·Statements·here]

References¶

[Insert·Reference·List·here]¶

Tables¶

[Insert·Tables·here.·Each·table·on·its·own·page.]¶

Figures¶

[Insert·Figures·here]¶

Figure·Legends¶

[Insert·Figure·Legends·here]¶

Modifying a Word Template

Word Templates that are delivered as content files included in the EndNote software are created with Microsoft Word. All these templates also incorporate *Macros* and *Wizards*. The templates can be customized in many ways and this instruction will describe how to modify page layout, paragraph styles (fonts, line spacing, indenting etc.), subject headings and alike. Certain structures of the EndNote Template collection must however be kept intact in order to allow the Wizard to work properly.

Most fields can also be changed, but the following fields are required and cannot be deleted:

[Insert Title of Article]

[Insert Names of Author(s)]

[Insert Corresponding Author information here**]**

[Insert Running Title <40 characters**]**

[Insert MeSH **Keywords** 3-10**]**

[Insert Reference List here**]**

[Insert Figure Legends here**]**

The Bold black text is compulsory whereas the grey text may be omitted or changed.

Creating a New Template

♦ **Follow These Steps**

1. Start Word.
2. Open an existing EndNote Word Template with **File - Open...** and navigate to EndNote's Template folder, normally C:\Program Files\EndNote\Templates.
3. Go to **File - Save As...** and save the new template with a new name in EndNote's Templates folder. Make sure that the document type is Document Template, *.dot.
4. The name of the new template will require an EndNote style with the same name. Example: Template *abc.dot* will require the EndNote style *abc.ens*.

Modifying the Welcome Screen

You can modify the welcome screen of the Wizard with your own text.

♦ **Follow These Steps**

1. Start Word.
2. Open the template.
3. Go to **File - Properties**.
4. In the **<new template>.dot Properties** window select the **Summary** tab.
5. Type the name of the Journal (or the title you may use) in the **Title:** section.

6 In the **Comments:** section type the title again followed by a blank line. More information can be typed after the blank line.

Information that has been typed here will be displayed on the welcome page of the Wizard.

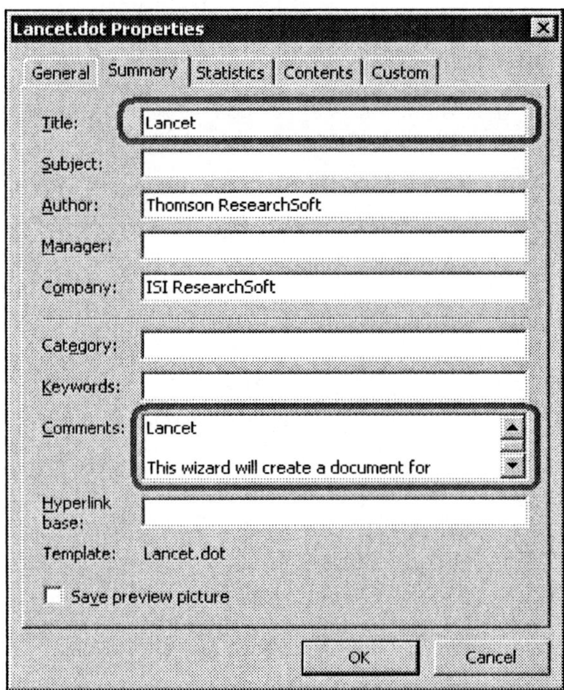

Creating a New Macro Field

When you need a new macro field the easiest way is to copy and paste an existing field and then modify it.

♦ **Follow These Steps**

1 Highlight an existing macro field.

2 Go to **Edit - Copy**
or key command **[Ctrl]** + **[C]**
or right-click the mouse and select **Copy**.

3 Move the cursor to the position you want to place the new macro and go to **Edit - Paste**
or **[Ctrl]** + **[V]**
or right-click the mouse and select **Paste**.

4 Place the cursor over the new macro field and right-click the mouse and select **Toggle Field Codes**.

5 The text within brackets [..] can now be changed as long as you leave the first word **Insert** intact as being the first word.

6 Highlight the new macro field and right-click the mouse and select **Toggle Field Codes**.

7 Go to **File - Save As...** and save the modified template with the same or a new name in EndNote's Templates folder. Make sure that the document type is Document Template, *.dot.

You have now created a new macro which will become an option in the Wizard under **Sections**.

Adding New Word (Paragraph) Styles

It is easy to add paragraph styles from existing templates or documents to your customized Word templates.

♦ **Follow These Steps**

1. Open the Word template that you want to modify.
2. Go to **Tools - Templates and Add-ins.**
3. Click on [**Organizer...**].

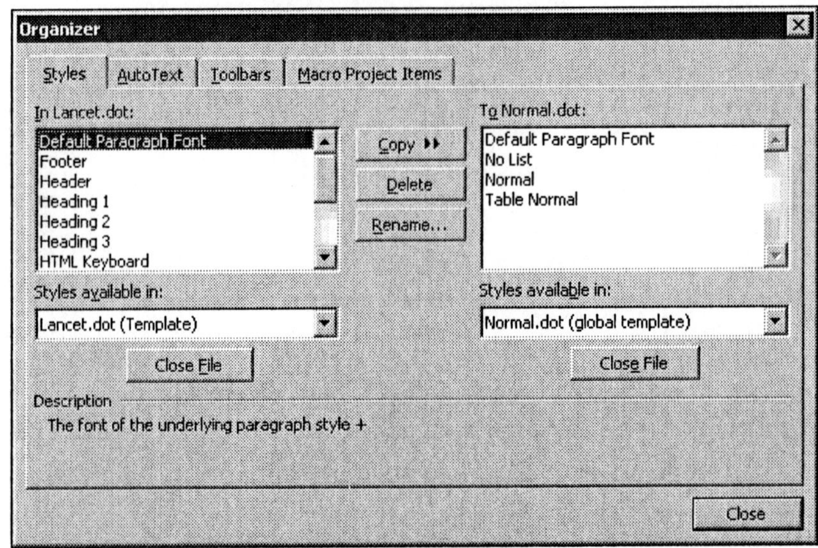

4. The **Styles** tab will allow you to copy paragraph styles from the associated documents to your active document. You can also close the Normal template with the [**Close File**]-button and when all files are closed then open a new document with [**Open File...**]. From the new document you can now copy any of its paragraph styles or other objects.

Finally, always test your modified templates. Make sure the templates are saved as a *.dot file and are located in the EndNote template folder. Remember also, that a corresponding Output Style with same file name as the template and with file extension *.ens must be available in EndNote's Styles folder.

Removing Field Codes from Documents Based on Word Templates

The preferred method of removing field codes from a document based on a Word Template from EndNote's collection is the manual method based on Word's generic command [**Ctrl**] + [**A**], [**Ctrl**] + [**6**] as described on page 90. Using EndNote's native command **Remove Field Codes** normally causes linking to the selected template to be replaced by the default template Normal.dot and you may loose most of the paragraph styles and other document settings that you have selected.

APPENDIX A - KEY COMMANDS

Listed below are some of the most useful key commands. Many of these strictly adhere to general Windows conventions. Some are specific for each program.

Windows	Word	EndNote	Key Commands	Description
✔	✔	✔	[Ctrl] + [C]	Copy
		✔	[Ctrl] + [K]	Copy Formatted
✔	✔	✔	[Ctrl] + [X]	Cut
✔	✔	✔	[Ctrl] + [V]	Paste
✔	✔	✔	[Ctrl] + [A]	Select/Unselect All
✔	✔	✔	[Ctrl] + [O]	Open Document/Library
		✔	[Ctrl] + [F]	Search References
		✔	[Ctrl] + [M]	Show All References
		✔	[Ctrl] + [PgUp]	Previous Reference
		✔	[Ctrl] + [PgDn]	Next Reference
		✔	[Ctrl] + [J]	Go To
	✔		[Ctrl] + [G]	Go To
		✔	[Ctrl] + [G]	Open Link
✔	✔	✔	[Ctrl] + [N]	New Document/Reference
		✔	[Ctrl] + [E]	Edit References
		✔	[Ctrl] + [D]	Delete References
✔	✔	✔	[Ctrl] + [P]	Print Document/References
✔	✔	✔	[Ctrl] + [S]	Save
		✔	[Ctrl] + [Q]	Exit Program
		✔	[Ctrl] + [1]	Open List
		✔	[Ctrl] + [3]	Link Term Lists
		✔	[Ctrl] + [4]	Define Term Lists
✔	✔	✔	[Ctrl] + [W]	Close Window
✔	✔	✔	[Ctrl]+[Shift]+[W]	Close all Windows of same Type
		✔	[Ctrl] + [Y]	Spell Check
	✔	✔	[Ctrl] + [Z]	Undo
	✔		[Ctrl] + [B]	Find
	✔		[Ctrl] + [H]	Replace
		✔	[Ctrl] + [R]	Change Text

Windows	Word	EndNote	Key Commands	Description
	✓[31]	✓	**[Alt] + [1]**	Toggle between EndNote/Word
	✓[31]	✓	**[Alt] + [2]**	Insert Citation(s)
	✓[31]	✓	**[Alt] + [3]**	Format Bibliography
	✓[31]		**[Alt] + [4]**	Unformat Citation(s)
	✓[31]		**[Alt] + [5]**	Show/Edit Library Reference(s)
	✓[31]		**[Alt] + [6]**	Edit Citation(s)
	✓[31]		**[Alt] + [7]**	Find Citation(s)
	✓[31]	✓	**[Alt] + [8]**	Import/Export Traveling Library
	✓[31]	✓	**[Alt] + [9]**	CWYW Preferences
	✓[31]		**[Alt] + [0]**	Insert Note
	✓		**[Ctrl] + [6]**	Unlink Fields
		✓	**[Shift] + [F4]**	Window - Cascade
		✓	**[Shift] + [F5]**	Window - Tile
	✓		**[Ctrl]+[Alt]+[F]**	Insert Footnote

[31] The combination of EndNote 7 and Word XP carries an imperfection so that some key commands from Word do not work. The EN7CWYW.dot file in Word's startup folder must be replaced. Consult your support.

APPENDIX B – FILE TYPES USED BY ENDNOTE

Programfiles:

- ENDNOTE.EXE (program file)
- NETSETUP.EXE (installs search paths in a network)
- EN7CWYW.WLL (CWYW for Word 97)
- ENα[32]CWYW.WLL (CWYW for Word 2000)
- ENαCWYW.WordXP.WLL (CWYW for Word 2002 or 2003)
- ENαCWYW.DOT

Files, created and used by EndNote:

- *.ENL (EndNote Library)
- *.ENF (EndNote Filter)
- *.ENZ (EndNote Connection File)
- *.ENS (EndNote Style)
- *.ENQ (EndNote Query, EndNote search history)
- RefTypeTable.XML (for EndNote 9, see page 29)

Import file formats:

- *.* structured text format, needs filter
- *.ENW (includes the %-tags) EndNote Import option
- *.CIW (ISI Common Export format) ISI-CE Import option
- *.OVD (OVIDs and SilverPlatter's Direct Export format) requires filters
- *.RIS (RIS Direct Export format) RIS Import option
- *.* other structured file formats

Export file formats:

- *.TXT
- *.ENW (text file, created with *EndNote Export.ENS*)
- *.RTF
- *.HTM
- *.XML

Other text files:

- CONNECT.LOG
- *.TXT (export from/import to term list)
- *.TLX (dictionary file format)

Some EndNote-files are defined during the installation so that a Run command or a double-click activates the following procedures:

- *.ENL - EndNote starts and the library opens
- *.ENF - EndNote starts and the filter opens for editing
- *.ENZ - EndNote starts and connects to destination
- *.ENS - EndNote starts and the style opens for editing
- *.ENW - EndNote starts and activates direct import
- *.CIW - EndNote starts and activates direct import (Common format also for Reference Manager and ProCite)
- *.OVD - EndNote starts and activates direct import (Common format also for Reference Manager and ProCite)
- *.RIS - EndNote starts and activates direct import (Common format also for Reference Manager and ProCite)

[32] Where α represents 7, 8, 9, or X depending on the EndNote-version.

APPENDIX C – FLOW CHART

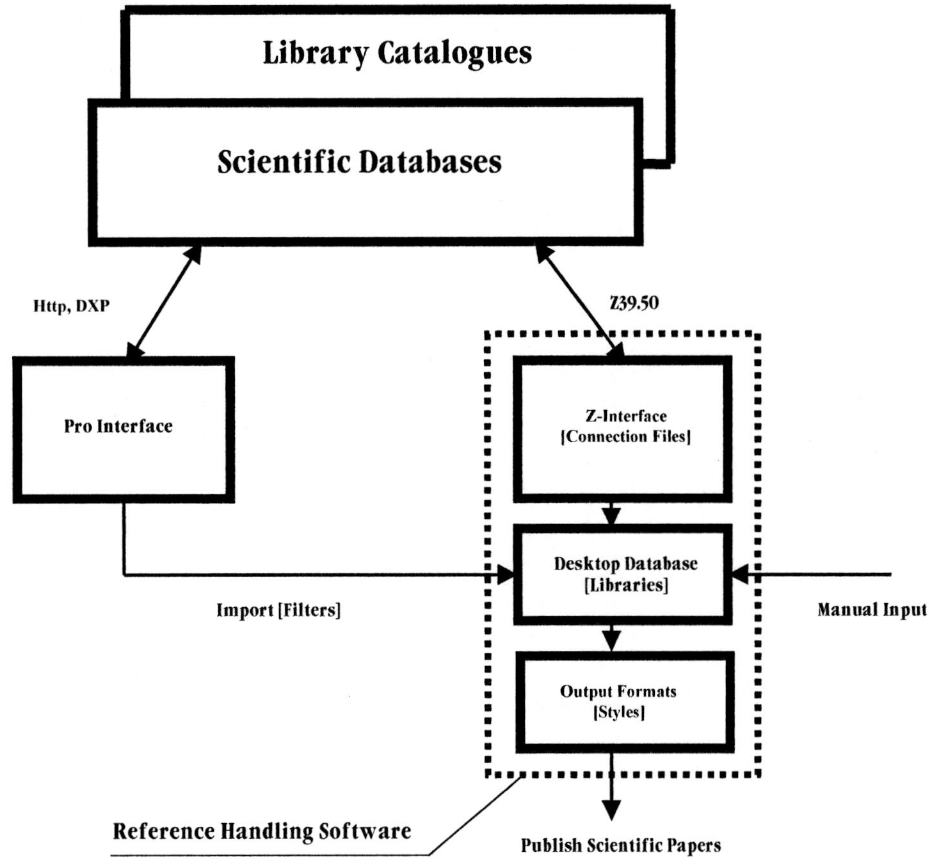

The following options are available for the transfer of records to an EndNote library.

1. Online search and retrieval with EndNote operating as client software (Z-Interface). *Requires one unique connection file per database.*
2. Download of a textfile by means of a Web-browser (Pro Interface) followed by an import through a filter. *Requires one unique filter per database.*
3. Direct Export is a special download format. The host creates a file that will start EndNote with a preselected standard filter. *The user needs only to select the import target.* This method is used by i.a. Web of Science, Ovid, WebSPIRS, EBSCO but presently not by PubMed.
4. Manual typing of data. Use **References** - **New Reference** or key command **[Ctrl]** + **[N]** and an empty reference form will be displayed.

APPENDIX D - GRAPHIC CONVENTIONS

In this book we have applied some simple graphic conventions with the intention to improve the readability and make the material easier to understand.

Example	Comments
Go to **References - New Reference**	Main menu and submenus in **Bold**
Choose **Layout** tab	Alternative tabs in **Bold**
Select **Field Shading:** *Always*	Variable in **Bold,** value in *Italic.* Subject in **Bold**, option in *Italic*
Confirm with [**Open**]	Graphic button uses brackets
Use [**Del**]-key to delete	Keyboard key uses brackets
Type **`Bibliography`** in the textbox	**`Courier`** font for typed text
..`[1-3]` will display	**`Courier`** font for displayed text
..or key command [**Alt**] + [**1**]	Hold the first key while touching the second

INDEX

SUPPORT AGREEMENT & PROPRIETARY FILES

Thank you for buying this book. You may or may not be aware that email support is available with this book. Should you have bought all three books in the series (*PubMed Essentials*, *PubMed and EndNote*, and *Manuscript Handling Using EndNote and Word*) you are now entitled to one year's free email support.

The support agreement is as follows:

This support is limited to an email service based around subjects covered in the books. It also entitles you to updated propriety files for EndNote (Form & Kunskap's connection files, import filters and output styles) should they have been modified since your purchase. Responses to support questions will normally be in the form of an email which will specify how to fix the problem by for example quoting a page number of a particular book or other suggestions.

Should you require assistance with creating or customising, connection files, import filters or output styles then this is defined as consultancy work. We are happy to provide assistance with this type of work but it will attract an additional charge. You will be informed of this when this type of work is requested and our charges will then be laid out in the form of a quotation.

The Proprietary Files and the online Registration Form are available at the following URL, which is restricted to holders of these books:

http://www.formkunskap.com/register
User ID: **pmen**
Password: **1943**

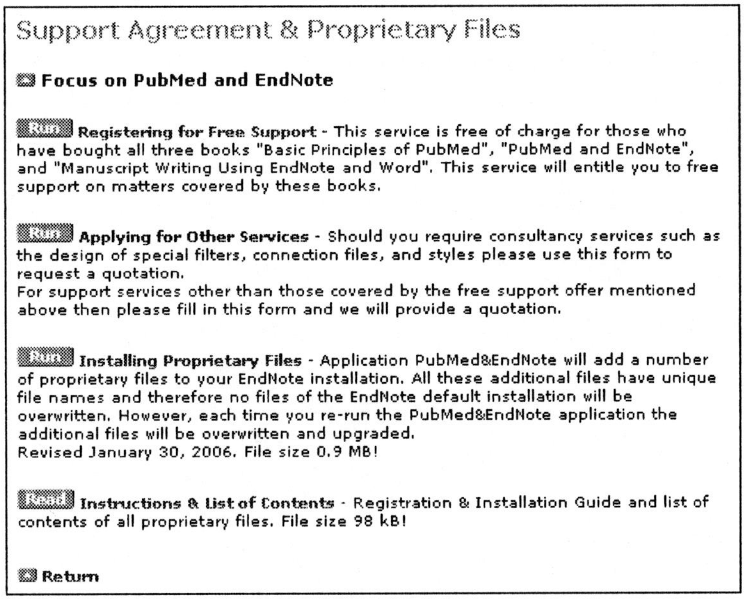

Support Agreement & Proprietary Files

Focus on PubMed and EndNote

Run **Registering for Free Support** - This service is free of charge for those who have bought all three books "Basic Principles of PubMed", "PubMed and EndNote", and "Manuscript Writing Using EndNote and Word". This service will entitle you to free support on matters covered by these books.

Run **Applying for Other Services** - Should you require consultancy services such as the design of special filters, connection files, and styles please use this form to request a quotation.
For support services other than those covered by the free support offer mentioned above then please fill in this form and we will provide a quotation.

Run **Installing Proprietary Files** - Application PubMed&EndNote will add a number of proprietary files to your EndNote installation. All these additional files have unique file names and therefore no files of the EndNote default installation will be overwritten. However, each time you re-run the PubMed&EndNote application the additional files will be overwritten and upgraded.
Revised January 30, 2006. File size 0.9 MB!

Read **Instructions & List of Contents** - Registration & Installation Guide and list of contents of all proprietary files. File size 98 kB!

Return

Registering for Free Support

Registering for Free support will display the following form:

REGISTRATION FOR FREE SUPPORT FOR THOSE WHO HAVE BOUGHT ALL THREE BOOKS LISTED BELOW. PLEASE PROVIDE ALL THREE ISBN NUMBERS:

Name: (*)

Title, position:

Address/University/Organization State/Province/Country: (*)

E-mail: (*)

"Basic Principles of PubMed": (*)

"PubMed and EndNote": (*)

"Manuscript Writing..": (*)

Where or from whom did you buy these books?: (*)

Comments:

Register Clear

Fields marked with an asterisk (*) are compulsory.

Return

After completing the form click the **[Register]**-button. We will confirm your registration with an e-mail with a Support Registration Code (which you must refer to in the correspondance) within three working days.

Installing the Proprietary Files

Installing the Proprietary Files requires *Admin properties.* Uninstalling can be made with the Control Panel.

To install the Proprietary Files please ensure that EndNote has been sucessfully installed prior to running this program. By selecting **[Run] 'Installing Proprietary Files'** the program will start and following message should appear:

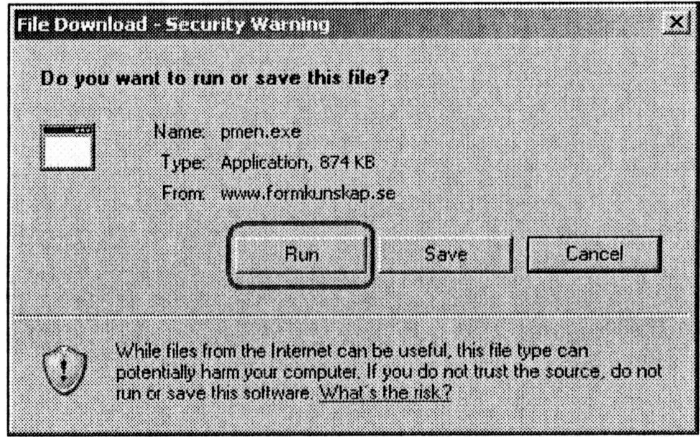

Click on the **[Run]**-button and the installation will commence.

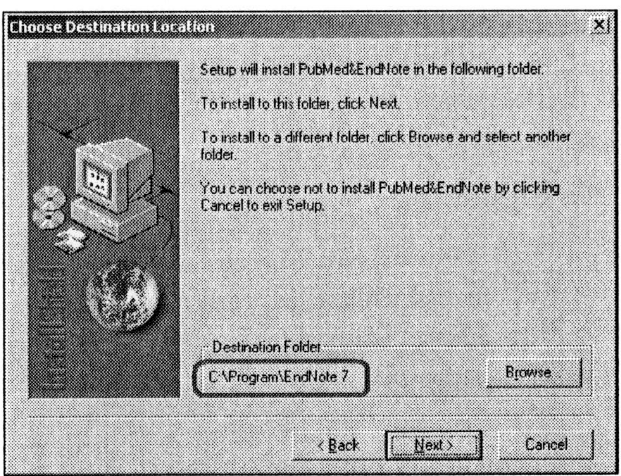

Check that the destination folder is correct. If so, then click on **[Next]**. When the installation is completed you will have a confirmation message.

Proprietary Files - List of Contents

The proprietary files are organized in a folder structure which conforms with your existing program installation. However, each file name is unique which ensures that none of the original files are overwritten.

1. **..\EndNote\Show_Blue_Eng.pdf, ..\EndNote\Show_Blue_Swe.pdf**
Introduction to Informatics and Terminologies - Slide Show (PDF). Next with **[Enter]** or **[PgDn]**, previous with **[PgUp]**. Discontinue with **[Esc]**.

2. **..\EndNote\Connections\BURK.enz**
Connection File for Burk, owned by BTJ, Lund. Free access.

3. **..\EndNote\Connections\MIKS.enz**
Connection File for the Library of Karolinska Institute. Free access.

4. **..\EndNote\Connections\PUBMEDGM.enz**
Connection File for PubMed, owned and administered by the National Library of Medicine. Free access.

5. **..\EndNote\Filters\A AMED (OVID).enf**
Filter for direct import from AMED (OVID).

6. **..\EndNote\Filters\A CINAHL (OVID).enf**
Filter for direct import from CINAHL (OVID).

7. **..\EndNote\Filters\A EMBASE (OVID).enf**
Filter for direct import from EMBASE (OVID).

8. **..\EndNote\Filters\A GLOBAL HEALTH (OVID).enf**
Filter for direct import from GLOBAL HEALTH (OVID).

9. **..\EndNote\Filters\A MEDLINE (OVID).enf**
Filter for direct import from Medline (OVID).

10. **..\EndNote\Filters\A OLDMED (OVID).enf**
Filter for direct import from Oldmedline (OVID).

11. **..\EndNote\Filters\A PREMED (OVID).enf**
Filter for direct import from Premedline (OVID).

12. ..\EndNote\Filters\A PsycINFO (OVID).enf
Filter for direct import from PsycINFO (OVID).

13. ..\EndNote\Filters\A WebSPIRS (OVID).enf
Filter for direct import from WebSPIRS (OVID).

14. ..\EndNote\Filters\Cochrane (InterScience).enf
Filter for import from Cochrane Library on InterScience.

15. ..\EndNote\Filters\PUBMEDGM.enf
Filter for import from PubMed on the web.

16. ..\EndNote\Filters\SveMed_Plus(BRS).enf
Filter for import from SveMed Plus (BRS) at KIB on the web.

17. ..\EndNote\Styles\KIB_Order.ens
Style for ordering of documents from KIB. Only selected fields (with field labels).

18. ..\EndNote\Styles\Print_Abstract.ens
Style for easy reading of abstracts in the Preview-window of an EndNote library.

19. ..\EndNote\Styles\Print_All.ens
Style for easy reading of printout of all fields (with field labels) of selected records.

20. ..\EndNote\Styles\Print_Order.ens
Style for document ordering. Only selected fields (with field labels).

21. ..\EndNote\Styles\Print_PMID.ens
Style for ordering of documents by means of PMID.

22. ..\EndNote\Styles\PUBMEDGM_Export.ens
Style that restores the PubMed Citation link.

23. ..\EndNote\Styles\Tab Delimited EN7 Excel.ens
Style for EndNote 7 and earlier and export to Excel.

24. ..\EndNote\Styles\Tab Delimited EN8 Excel.ens
Style for EndNote 8 and later and export to Excel.

25. ..\EndNote\Templates\EndNote7.xlt
Excel-template for EndNote 7 and earlier.

26. ..\EndNote\Templates\EndNote8.xlt
Excel-template for EndNote 8 and later.

27. ..\EndNote\Term_Lists\Med_aim.txt
EndNote term list with alternative journal names for subset Abridged Index Medicus. Matches 'jsubsetaim' in **Any Field.**

28. ..\EndNote\Term_Lists\Med_dent.txt
EndNote term list with alternative journal names for subset Index to Dental Literature. Matches 'jsubsetd' in **Any Field.**

29. ..\EndNote\Term_Lists\Med_health.txt
EndNote term list with alternative journal names for Health Care Administration (HealthSTAR). Matches 'jsubseth' in **Any Field.**

30. ..\EndNote\Term_Lists\Med_medline.txt
EndNote term list with alternative journal names for Index Medicus, corresponding to virtually all journals indexed in Medline.

31. ..\EndNote\Term_Lists\Med_nurs.txt
EndNote term list with alternative journal names for International Nursing Index. Matches 'jsubsetn' in **Any Field.**

Printed in the United States
63110LVS00006B/23

9 781411 688391